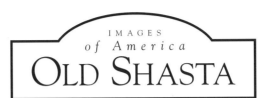

IMAGES
of America

OLD SHASTA

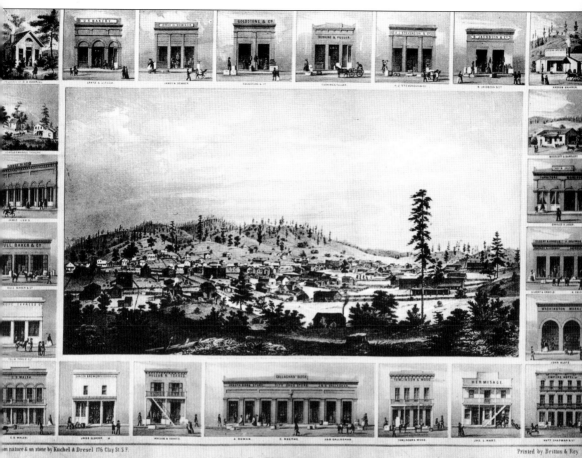

SHASTA, 1856.
SHASTA COUNTY, CALIFORNIA.

This lithograph, titled "Shasta, 1856," was entered in the clerk's office of the United States District Court for the Northern District of California, according to an Act of Congress by Anton Roman. Drawn from nature and on stone by Kuchel and Dresel, this lithograph depicts businesses and some residences in gold-rush Shasta.

ON THE COVER: By 1895, the Litsch Store was the only remaining gold-rush business in existence in Shasta.

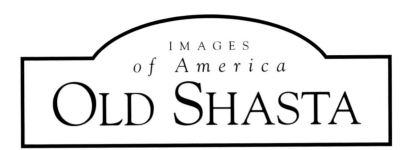

IMAGES
of America
OLD SHASTA

Town of Shasta Interpretive Association
with Al M. Rocca, Ph.D.

ARCADIA

Copyright © 2005 by Town of Shasta Interpretive Association
ISBN 0-7385-3094-8

Published by Arcadia Publishing
Charleston SC, Chicago IL, Portsmouth NH, San Francisco CA

Printed in Great Britain

Library of Congress Catalog Card Number: 2005934844

For all general information contact Arcadia Publishing at:
Telephone 843-853-2070
Fax 843-853-0044
E-mail sales@arcadiapublishing.com
For customer service and orders:
Toll-Free 1-888-313-2665

Visit us on the Internet at www.arcadiapublishing.com

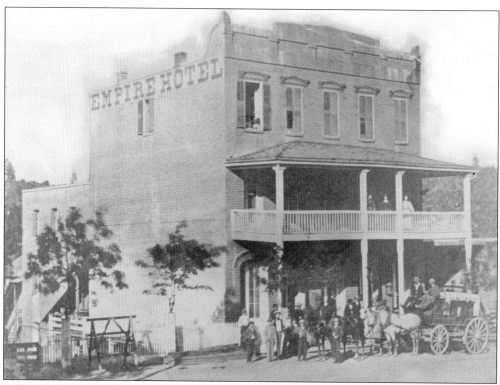

Advertised as a first-class establishment, the Empire Hotel served the Shasta community for over 63 years, from 1857 to 1920. The owners and operators included such notable Shastans as John V. Scott, Thomas Greene, Charles Behrens, and James J. Hill.

CONTENTS

ACKNOWLEDGMENTS

This book is possible because of the rich archives preserved by the California Department of Parks and Recreation at Shasta State Historic Park, and the writing talents of Prof. Al Rocca. We also wish to recognize the past staff members, volunteers, and donors who contributed to the archives and to identify those individuals who participated directly with this particular publication.

Those individuals who have shared our great appreciation and support for the colorful history of Shasta, and therefore devoted themselves to this book, are as follows, in alphabetical order: Linda Cooper, museum curator; Janet Howard, park interpretive specialist; Jack Frost, guide; Bruce Lynn, state park superintendent; Lori Martin, ranger; and Joseph Zeno, park aide. These people and, of course, Professor Rocca took that step outside the box and added this formidable task to their daily routines.

We are also grateful that in the process of producing this book, the museum archives were improved, and fresh historical information was found, enhancing the interpretive and preservation value of the park.

And finally, who are "we?" We are the Town of Shasta Interpretive Association. This is a nonprofit organization whose main mission is to raise funds that support school group visitation, special events, and park programs that we believe inspire people to recall the origins of Shasta's history. Indeed, Shasta was once called Redding Springs, Shasta City, the Town of Shasta, and we know her familiarly today as Old Shasta.

Please know that by purchasing this book, you too have contributed to the preservation and support of Shasta State Historic Park. We cordially invite you to become a member of the Town of Shasta Interpretive Association. Our membership information is located at www.parks.ca.gov.

—Bert Aarsen, President
Town of Shasta Interpretive Association

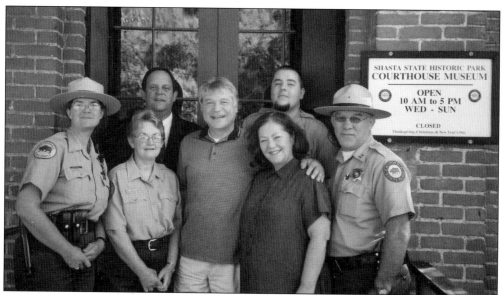

Those who worked on this book, pictured from to left to right, are Lori Martin, Janet Howard, Jack Frost, Al Rocca, Linda Cooper, Joe Zeno, and Bruce Lynn.

INTRODUCTION

Shasta became the site of California's second gold strike in 1848 when the area's only white settler, Pierson B. Reading, discovered gold in and around Clear Creek, after visiting Sutter's original gold strike near Coloma. News traveled fast when gold was mentioned, and it only took a few months before footloose, gold-hungry men—mostly bachelors—poured into the creeks and streams of Shasta County. One of those sites, Reading Springs, became a gathering place for water and rest. It was here that the town of Shasta started, when a few enterprising miners realized that they could make more money supplying the needs of the miners than actually mining.

Naming their new gold-mining boomtown for nearby majestic Mount Shasta, town leaders like John Mackley and Karl Augustus Grotefend became successful hotel owners, encouraging others to invest in business. Mercantiles, drugstores, livery stables, and bakeries sprang up, and more and more miners flooded into the town. By 1850, a rut-ridden dirt road linked Shasta with towns to the south, all the way to Sacramento. Daily stagecoaches brought the mail and visitors, while flatbed wagons delivered lumber, tools, clothing, furniture, shoes, and food supplies.

A quick look at the 1850 census reveals that Shasta was truly a cosmopolitan town, with miners arriving from all parts of the Eastern United States, Europe, and a large contingent of Chinese. For the most part, these gold seekers lived peacefully together except for the occasional gold-claim dispute or a "friendly" disagreement over cards. Townspeople elected sheriffs, judges, and established a court of sessions to establish law and order. Whenever a murder occurred, the entire town came out for the trial and, if necessary, the hanging. Such was the case of Alexander Higgins, found guilty of killing his partner with an axe in 1855.

By 1853, the town's population revealed more women and children, and the feel of a permanent community began to surface. By this time, Benoni Whitten had applied for state funding to open the first school. While this school did not last long, others stepped forward and with the help of local churches, classes continued. The first place of worship, a Methodist church, began Sunday services in 1852 and was quickly followed by a Catholic church the next year.

The town survived several ravaging fires that, each time, consumed most or all of the wooden businesses and homes. The reason for such destruction is simple—the structures were built extremely close to one another, and in many cases, shared a common wall. After the 1853 conflagration, business leaders rebuilt with brick, at great expense. And so the town continued to grow. Baseball teams flourished and special events, such as holiday celebrations, races, and "street entertainment" all helped to ingrain a sense of community.

By 1860, the economic trends were beginning to reveal less profits and business activity. Much of this was due to the decline of new mining claims and the fact that miners had "played out" the easy gold and were moving to new claims out of the area. However, the town still "ruled" as the main regional business center and townspeople saw a bright future

Everything changed in 1872, when officials with Southern Pacific Railroad became determined to build a connection that would link Sacramento with the newly established towns of the northern valley. Shasta citizens assumed that this would mean that the railroad would find its terminus in their town. But that was not to be. Railroad engineers decided to only come as far as the topographic head of the Sacramento Valley, where the Sacramento River turns west into a steep canyon. This location, known to the local inhabitants as Poverty Flats, was about five miles from the town of Shasta. It might as well have been 50 miles away, for instead of enhancing the growth of Shasta, the railroad initiated the final collapse of the former gold-mining boomtown.

Poverty Flats became the town of Redding, and immediately Shasta residents began moving to the new town, taking advantage of cheap building lots and access to the railroad. Not everyone moved at once, but by 1880, Shasta's population was clearly on the decline. Entrepreneurs like Chauncey Carroll Bush did not wait long to move, as he set up the first mercantile store in

Redding. He became very successful in his new business location and convinced other business owners to join him.

A turning point for Shasta's future came again in 1882, when civic leaders in Redding decided that the time had come to seize the county seat from Shasta. The battle was on, and Shasta residents rallied to help save their town. Citizens realized that if the county seat left their town, numerous jobs and county money would leave forever. The results of the election revealed that Shasta had retained the county seat, but only by a small margin. Redding civic leaders did not give up and in the 1886 election they prevailed. The county moved to Redding in 1888 and Shasta residents fumed over their defeat.

Despite the loss of the county seat, Shasta remained a viable community as the decades wore on. Hopes for economic revival sprouted off and on, such as the 1890–1920 explosion of copper mining and smelting activity. Yet new towns were created close to the mines, such as Ingot and Kennett and little of the new money found its way to Shasta. With the decline of the copper industry during the 1920s, following the end of World War I, a general depression hit the county and more people moved from the area. Even the construction of a paved road from Redding to Shasta and points west did not help the economy. Neither did the building of Shasta Dam in the late 1930s and early 1940s. By this time, most of the remaining commercial buildings in Shasta stood vacant and crumbling.

It was during this time that individuals stepped forward to save the historic gold-rush town. Led by Mae Helene Bacon Boggs, concerned Shasta county residents worked with state officials to designate the town as an historic landmark and to preserve the site. By 1950, the California State Parks Commission purchased land and began a restoration of some of the remaining buildings, such as the main courthouse.

Today the town of Shasta is a community of several hundred residents, but a portion of it is an official state historic park. Located off Highway 299, Shasta State Historic Park shares gold-rush history with thousands of visitors each year and provides ongoing educational programs to the area's local schools and other organizations.

One

CHANGE IN THE SPIRIT
OF THE LAND

The Native Americans of Shasta County lived in harmony with the challenging local environment for thousands of years. In the area west of the city of Redding, in canyons and meadows near creeks that feed into the Sacramento River, possibly a few thousand American Indians resided peacefully. They were, and are, members of the Wintun tribe. Alternative spellings and names for this tribe include Wintoons, Keniesti, and Patawe. Their language, belonging to the Penutian cluster of dialects, was spoken in much of the Sacramento Valley. However, it should be noted that significant dialect variations existed between tribes. The neighbors of the Wintuns included the Yana in the eastern foothills, the Shastans to the north, and the Achomawi in the northeast mountains. All of these tribes spoke versions of the Hokan linguistic group.

Life for the American Indians proved to be a constant challenge to find and preserve food and to maintain shelter. Fish and acorns provided the staple food supply of the Wintuns, along with hunting deer and small game. With fishing nets fashioned from tree branches and vines, the Wintuns successfully trapped trout and salmon along the nearby Sacramento River. Oak acorns were gathered by hardworking women and children, leached, then beaten into a meal bread or tortilla-type of food wrap, but sometimes eaten plain. Long stretches of berry bushes hugged both sides of nearby creeks and families spent hours picking berries from the thorny plants. Animal furs and skins, scraped clean and trimmed, provided clothing for the entire family. Hot summers forced most American Indians to shed their full-length skin coverings for less clothing, while the frequent cold, rainy winters required individuals to wrap themselves in additional animal skin blankets.

The hardy, persevering Wintuns used all of the local environment to ensure their survival. Many of their cultural practices and beliefs related, in one way or another, to the land and their interaction with it. Their basket making is an outstanding example of combining utility with art. These baskets, woven in a variety of sizes and shapes, held their food, tools, and ornaments. Wintuns made use of the deciduous trees and oaks to fashion weapons, such as spears, bows, and arrows. Young men were taught how to fashion a canoe from a single log and how to construct temporary lean-to shelters.

Wintun society centered its traditions on the family and the clan. Major events, which were joyously celebrated, included births and marriages. Newly married couples usually continued to live in their same clan, although when clans became large—over 50 individuals—it was not uncommon to have some member split away to live nearby in a new village.

Generations of Wintuns prospered in the Shasta area until the arrival of the white man, beginning with the short visit of one of America's most famous trappers and continental explorers, Jedediah Strong Smith. In 1826, Smith had been the first American to cross California's Sierra Nevada Mountains. Mexican authorities, fearing American intervention on their lands, quickly ordered Smith and his fellow trappers to leave the province. He did leave, but only for a short time. Smith was back in California the next year, only this time Mexican officials arrested him in Monterey. Promising once again to leave California, Smith procured horses and food and headed north up the Buenaventura (Sacramento) River. The plans called for his expedition to head up the valley and seek a "fur route" to British-controlled Fort Vancouver, on the north shore of the Columbia River.

By 1828, Smith followed the Sacramento River into what is now Shasta County. Somewhere in the southern part of the county, probably at Cottonwood Creek, Smith found the lowlands flooded and made the decision to head over to the coast. His probable route followed the middle fork of Cottonwood Creek west to the Platina-Beegum Gorge and on over into Trinity County via Wildwood Summit. From here, he could have traveled northwest on Hayfork Creek, then on the South Fork of the Trinity River, the Klamath River, and on to the coast. In later years, Smith commented, "I wanted to be the first to view a country on which the eyes of a white man had never gazed and to follow the course of rivers that run through a new land."

Exhausted and low on supplies, Smith remained as a guest at Fort Vancouver. While there, he gave accounts of the fine trapping grounds south of Oregon. British trappers had ventured south into Oregon on many occasions, but none had penetrated to California's Central Valley. News of the available new trapping lands in northern California spread and during the 1830s numerous hunting parties, British and American, visited Shasta County. Alexander McLeod hiked down from Fort Vancouver and followed the Sacramento River to the Bay Area in 1828–1829; followed by Peter Ogden in 1830, John Work in 1832–1833, and Michel LaFromboise in 1832. Work appears to have been everywhere in the northern part of the state during this time. His extensive explorations included surveying tributaries of the Sacramento River, blazing a trail to the sea via gaps in the lower coastal-range. Meanwhile Ewing Young recognized a financial opportunity when he decided to drive a herd of cattle up the Sacramento Valley, through the mountains, and on up to Fort Vancouver, where hard-to-get beef commanded high prices.

By 1840, northern California was becoming known to many Americans living in the East via stories told by experienced trappers and printed in numerous newspapers and books. One of the most widely read accounts of northern California was by trailblazer Langsford Hastings, who in 1843–1844 traversed the Sacramento River trail. He later published one of the most widely read books on Oregon and California, *Emigrants Guide to Oregon and California*. Most likely, he camped in or around Lower Soda Springs. Many of these tales spoke of the beautiful landscape, the mild climate, and the abundant game, but they said little about the hardships that would need to be endured. Naturally some of these East Coast readers yearned for the opportunity to find fame and fortune in a new land. One of these young men was Pierson Barton Reading.

Dwellings like this cedar bark house servd as both temporary and permanent housing. In the Shasta area, shards of tree trunks containing a layer of bark were used along with large branches to form a teepee-like structure.

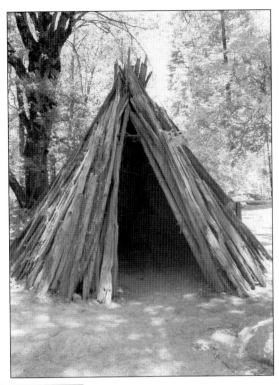

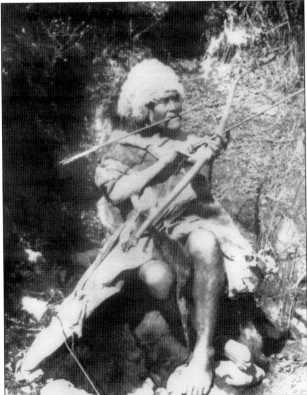

Khal-khoo-loo-li, a Wintu headman, encouraged his people to befriend settlers instead of driving them away. In this photograph, Khal-khoo-loo-li is clad in a mountain lion skin and armed with bow, arrows, and an animal-skin quiver.

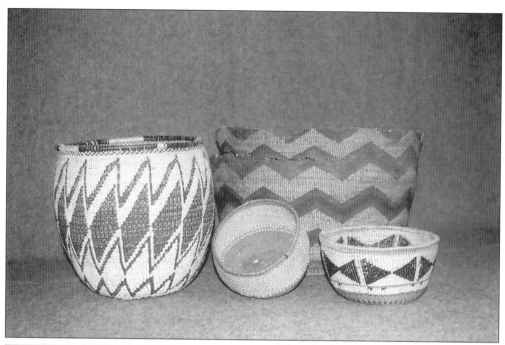

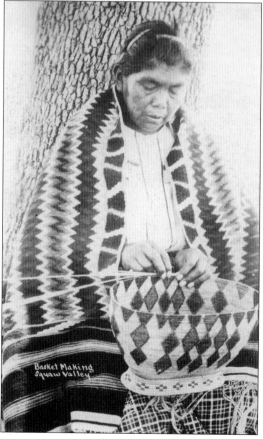

These baskets are examples from the permanent collection at Shasta State Historic Park. The basket at right in back is the remains of an unusually large Wintu storage basket. The warp is unidentified whole plant fiber shoots, and the weft is conifer root, with bear grass, woodwardia fern filaments dyed with alder bark, and maidenhair fern stem overlay. Strands of the weaver's hair can still be seen caught in the weave. This image of a Wintun woman is from an early postcard of the McCloud area.

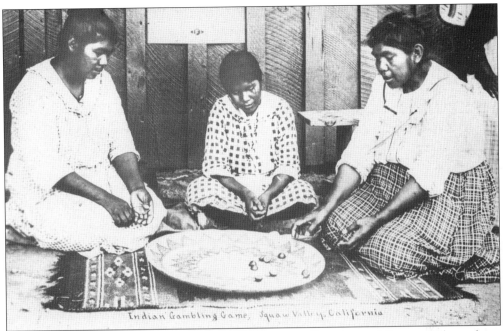

Foot races, wrestling matches, and jumping contests, as well as the gambling game shown here, were popular at Wintu gatherings.

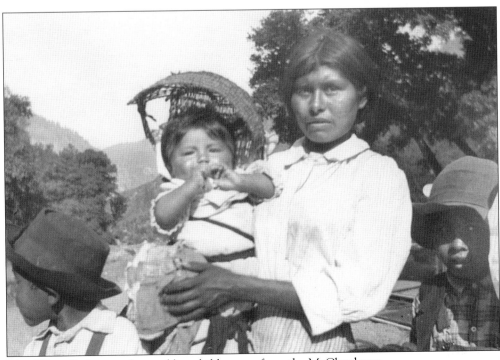

This Wintu Indian mother and her children are from the McCloud area.

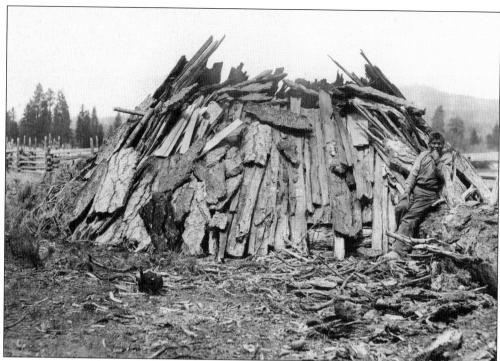

This is another example of a Wintu structure. These bark houses could have been made from cedar or ponderosa pine.

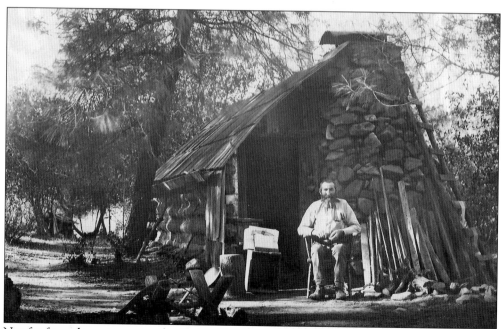

Not far from the entrance to the Union Cemetery lies the miner and baker, Nick Schumann. Marking his grave is a granite boulder upon which he sat to eat his lunch. His epitaph reads, "Born in Denmark 1823, Died 1901. This humble stone its vigil keeps and marks the spot where Schumann sleeps."

Advertising the superior accommodations to California, this 1849 travel poster represents the rush to the gold country. Overland travel was the only other method for reaching California.

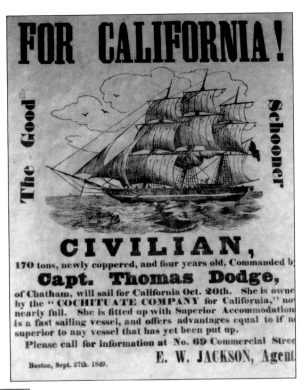

FOR CALIFORNIA!

The Good Schooner

CIVILIAN,

170 tons, newly coppered, and four years old, Commanded by

Capt. Thomas Dodge,

of Chatham, will sail for California Oct. 20th. She is owned by the " COCHITUATE COMPANY for California," now nearly full. She is fitted up with Superior Accommodation is a fast sailing vessel, and offers advantages equal to if no superior to any vessel that has yet been put up.

Please call for information at No. 69 Commercial Street

E. W. JACKSON, Agent

Boston, Sept. 27th. 1849.

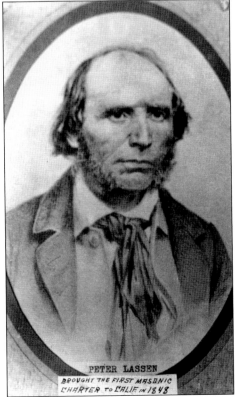

PETER LASSEN
BROUGHT THE FIRST MASONIC
CHARTER TO CALIF IN 1848

In 1848, Peter Lassen (1800–1859) opened up his "cut-off" from the Oregon emigrant route. This route allowed Lassen to provide the Masonic charter for the lodge in Shasta. Nearby Mount Lassen is named in recognition of his early efforts.

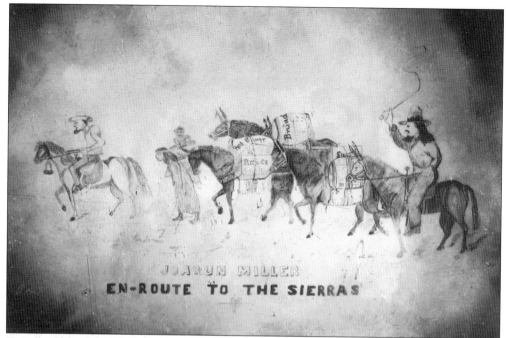

Travel to the gold fields by land was popular and affordable. Joaquin Miller left behind personal sketches in his journals. This print is dated 1853.

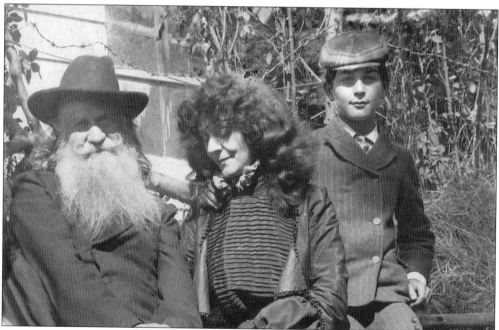

Pictured with his daughter and grandson is Joaquin Miller, or Cincinnatus Hiner Miller. Some consider him a historian on the clashes between the gold miners and indigenous American Indians. Mark Twain called him a liar. Miller spent a brief time jailed in Shasta for taking Thomas Bass's horse.

This landmark marks the point on Clear Creek where Major Reading and his Wintu workers mined and found gold. This site extended the gold fields 200 miles northward from John Sutter's discovery.

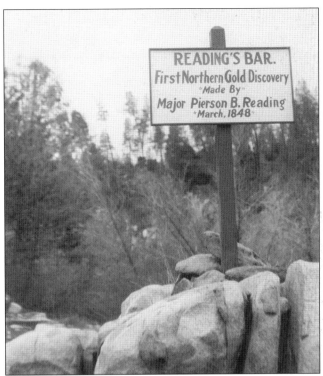

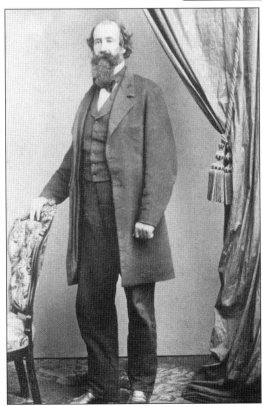

In May 1843, Pierson Barton Reading, a New Jersey native, joined a wagon train headed west. After arriving at Sutter's Fort in November, Reading was employed as a clerk by John Sutter. On Sutter's advice, Reading became a citizen of Mexico and applied for a land grant to be called Rancho Buena Ventura, near present-day Cottonwood. In 1856, Reading's title to the rancho was confirmed after the claim had been argued before the Supreme Court of the United States.

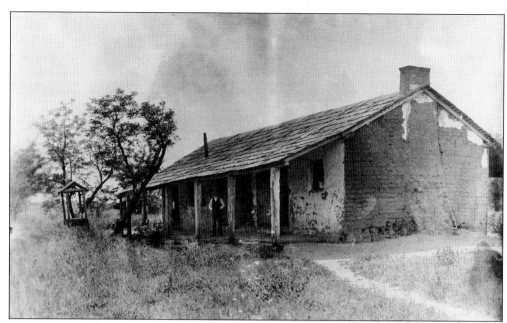

Built in 1847, this adobe was a first home for P. B. Reading. In 1850, the adobe briefly served as the first Shasta County seat. As Reading's family grew, a main house was added, and this portion served as the kitchen and servants quarters.

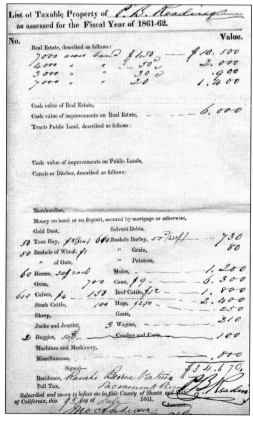

Items needed for maintaining Reading's Rancho Buena Ventura are itemized on the 1861–1862 list of taxable property at left.

Two

THE WORLD RUSHED TO SHASTA

Pierson Barton Reading, like many Americans at that time, followed the reports of the new wagon trains heading to California, such as the Bidwell-Bartleson Party of 1841. After careful consideration, he made the fateful decision to try his luck in California. "I had ever the desire to travel," he wrote. Reading signed on the Peter Burnett Party of wagon train families in May of 1843.

After arriving in Sacramento, John Sutter convinced Reading to apply for a land grant from the Mexican government. Reading, remembering the "beautiful northern valley," asked for, and received, a large parcel of land bordering both sides of the Sacramento River. He selected the name Buenaventura (good fortune) for his new rancho.

Before Reading could develop his large new rancho, trouble between Mexico and the United States led to the Bear Flag Revolt during the summer of 1846. Reading joined with other American rancho owners in open revolt against Mexican authority. He rose to the rank of major and was the first to sign the Treaty of Cahuenga, which ended Mexican military authority in California. Finally he was able to move to the Shasta area, where he built an adobe home not far from the present-day town of Cottonwood.

In 1848, John Sutter's millwright, James Marshall, discovered gold alongside the banks of the American River, near Coloma. Sutter tried desperately to keep the news of his gold strike a secret, and he only told a few close friends. One of those friends was Reading. Reading rode down, looked over the Coloma site, and quickly returned to Shasta, where he rounded up Wintu "workers" and promptly began panning Clear Creek (just outside of his rancho's western boundary) for gold. He did not have long to wait. Within the first few days of panning and digging, Reading found gold nuggets and dust in varying sizes and quality. This was California's second gold-rush site, whichbecame known as Reading's Bar, later Horsetown.

Failing to keep his gold strike a secret, Reading suddenly found his Clear Creek site flooded with hungry gold seekers. In response, Reading expanded his gold mining to the area a few miles north of Clear Creek. Here where water and shade were abundant, other miners soon followed. These early miners named the location Reading Upper Springs and it became a permanent campsite. By the winter of 1849–1850, prospectors used the camp as a gateway to the northern foothills and mountains. Within a short time, crude, handcrafted cabins dotted the hillsides. One of these early miners, Nick Shumann, known as "the hermit" by later Shasta residents, lived in the area until his death in 1901.

More and more miners moved to Reading Springs during the early months of 1850 and it became apparent to just about everyone that a town was in the making. Finally in June of that year, a meeting of townspeople considered a permanent name for their growing community. At first the name Fountania, alluding to the abundant water in the area, was suggested. In the end, the majority of miners voted for Shasta, a direct reference to the majestic mountain to their north.

That name had also just been designated for the county, as determined by new state legislature in 1849. Interestingly a committee of the legislature had named the area "Reading County" with boundaries from Red Bluff to the Oregon line and the coast ranges east to Nevada. However, on February 18, the name was changed to Shasta.

One early newspaper account, from October 7, 1850, gives an interesting look at the burgeoning new town and some of its earliest leaders.

> The people of Shasta c[C]ounty have never yet received the laws of the last legislature, and of course have to be a law unto themselves . . . Shasta City is considered the county seat, where the people met Sept. 14 and elected Dr. Robinson and Mr. Jones justices of the peace, and Mr. Oppenheimer, sheriff, which officers are successful in performing their duties and keeping good order. The town is squatter, each settler claiming 60 x 120 feet. It is exactly at the head of navigation—the ox-wag[g]on can go no further . . . The place has 35 stores, four or five families, half a dozen women only. A dry goods establishment would hardly do a driving business. Yet is seems flourishing, and is another proof of the capabilities of this great State to nourish a very large population even among its mountains.

Between 1849 and 1851, a significant trend developed that decided the direction the new town would take. The location of Reading Springs at first was a temporary campsite for gold seeking miners heading west and north to nearby creeks. As these creeks played out their gold, or became overcrowded, miners sought to expand their reach for diggings much further away, such as Trinity County and Siskiyou County. For extended trips into these remote locations, miners needed a reliable site to acquire substantial amounts of supplies to hold them over long periods of time. To satisfy this increasing need for tools, food, and clothing, the cabin town of Reading Springs was transformed into the commercial town of Shasta.

Many of the early residents of Shasta soon discovered that they could make much more money supplying the needs of miners than they could spending endless hours gold panning in cold creeks. Two excellent examples of this are Dr. Benjamin Shurtleff and Royal T. Sprague. Both men arrived in Shasta in 1849 as the town was just forming. Shurtleff, who had come to California via ship around Cape Horn, found that he could make money by opening a drugstore and mercantile business. He also practiced medicine. Sprague left his family in Ohio to come to the gold country. He made a good living practicing law, as there were ongoing land-claim disputes and lots of criminal cases to be handled.

Two immediate needs of the local miners were for lodging and supplies, and as noted in the newspaper account above, Shasta quickly answered the demand. A main street developed where most of the wood-framed buildings stood. Three hotels—the Globe, the St. Charles, and the Trinity House—garnered most of the early business from 1851 to 1853. Probably the most successful of the early stores was the R. J. Walsh Mercantile, which sold boots, tools, blankets, and other mining supplies as early as 1850.

Of course, the fate of the tiny boomtown depended on gold being found, and find gold they did. In 1851, the *Sacramento Union* newspaper reported that a company of seven miners from Shasta recovered $10,000 in just 15 days in nearby Whisky Creek. The largest single nugget assayed for over $900. A father and son team struck it rich, finding $8,000 in a period of one month. Most men did find some gold, and it was reported that the yield for a day's work averaged $25. All of this money needed to be spent somewhere and that somewhere, for the most part, was the town of Shasta. By 1853, the residents of Shasta saw a bright future indeed.

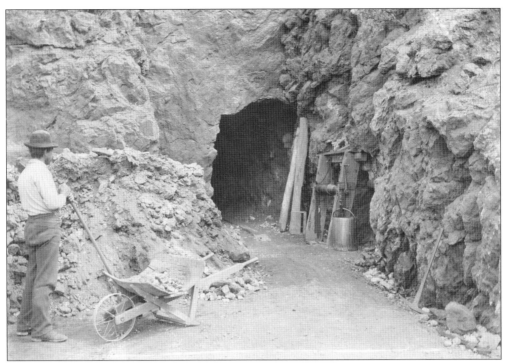

Leaving behind his family and a law practice in Ohio, Royal Tyler Sprague traveled overland to Shasta, arriving in 1849. He kept an absorbing journal for the three years he was separated from his family, detailing all aspects of mining and living during the gold rush. This is an image of Sprague's hard-rock mine.

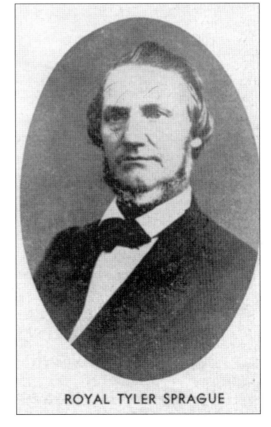

ROYAL TYLER SPRAGUE

Seeking gold quickly gave way to defending the accused in the court of the alcalde, Benjamin Shurtleff, and Royal T. Sprague acting as defense attorney. In 1852, having been the first to build a house on Shasta's Main Street, Sprague brought his beloved wife, Frank, and his children, Anna and Arthur, to make their home here. Serving four terms as an elected state senator, Sprague permanently moved to the state capitol in 1868. He served a 10-year term on the California Supreme Court and became the 21st chief justice in 1872. He died shortly thereafter.

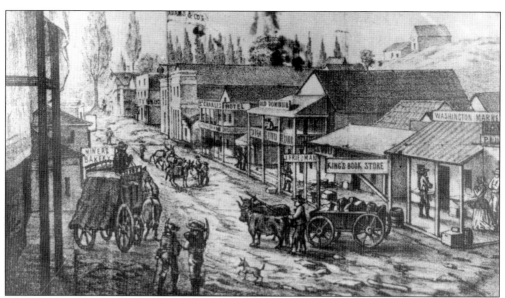

This image from an 1852 letter sheet is one of Main Street Shasta. Letter sheets, folded and sealed with wax, were used for stationery in the 19th century. This view southeast shows wood-frame buildings along the south side, and is the only picture of Grotefend's St. Charles Hotel.

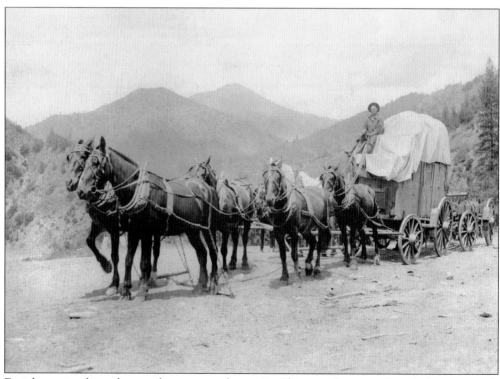

Freight trains brought supplies to merchants in Shasta, who transferred them to pack animals, that carried the supplies to the mines. This explains why Shasta became the hub of "whoa navigation."

Edward Ludwig Reese placer mined in the Rock Creek area as an early forty-niner. His name is included on the roll call of Lyons Light Infantry, formed in April 1861 to support the Union and protect the gold from Southern sympathizers.

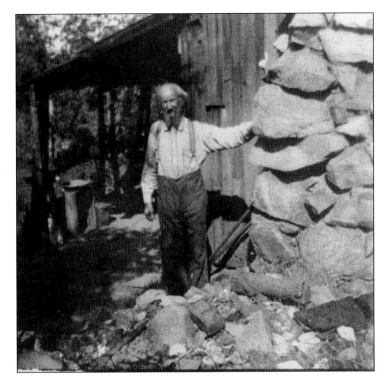

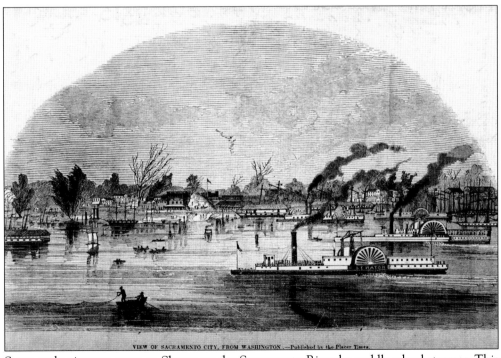

VIEW OF SACRAMENTO CITY, FROM WASHINGTON.—Published by the Placer Times.

Some early pioneers came to Shasta up the Sacramento River by paddle wheel steamer. This letter sheet image reflects such passage.

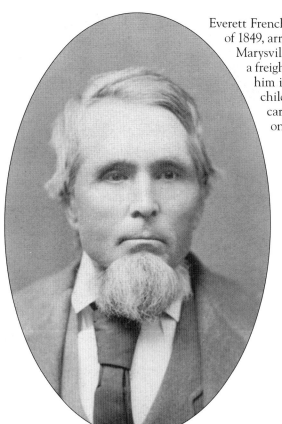

Everett French Crocker left Belfast, Ireland, in the fall of 1849, arriving in San Francisco in May 1850. From Marysville, he walked to Red Bluff and then took a freight wagon to Shasta. His wife, Mary, joined him in 1852 and taught school until their first child was born. Crocker was a bricklayer and carpenter, building an "up and down" sawmill on Rock Creek.

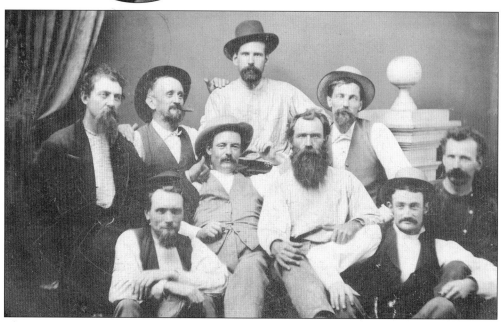

The "gentlemen" pictured here possibly "mined the miners" for their gold. Shasta had more than enough saloons to support any game of chance.

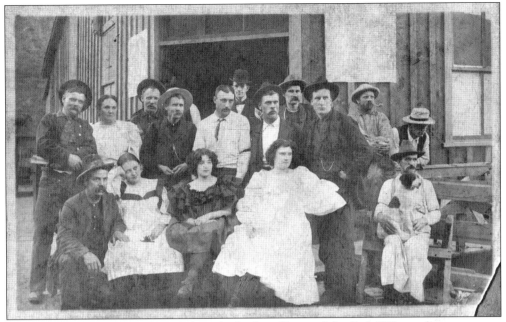

This photograph is simply identified on the back as "Some of the Girls." The earliest women to come west were not wives and mothers!

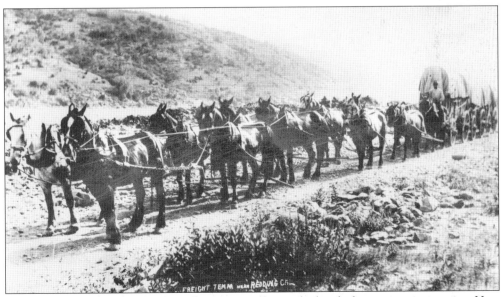

From 1849 to 1857, Shasta held the distinction of being the head of wagon transportation. Heat and dust were endured in the summer, great winds and torrents of rain in the winter. To reach Shasta was a mean, hard pull most of the way.

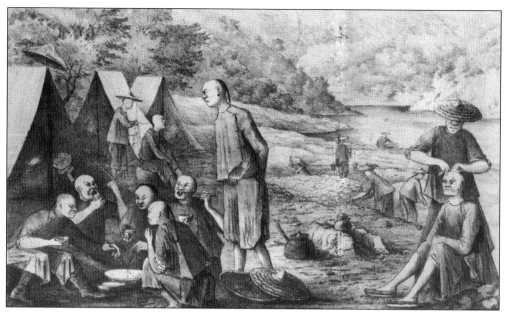

In 1853, Shasta had one of the largest Chinese populations in the state. Residing on the southern outskirts of Shasta, their "Hong Kong" consisted of a two-story hotel, stores, saloons, gambling dens, and a Joss House. Only the ruins of a brick prayer furnace on private property remain.

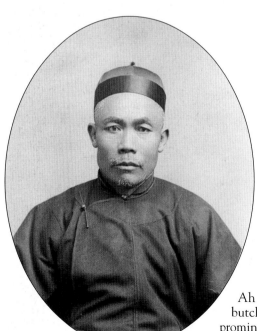

Ah Yem, also known as Big Yem, was a Chinese butcher in the early days of Shasta and, later, a prominent merchant with stores in San Francisco and China. He was also extensively engaged in mining.

In 1852, the Foreign Miner's Tax, passed by California legislators and aimed primarily at the Chinese, required all "aliens ineligible for citizenship" to pay a monthly fee. The Chinese were resented, disliked, and largely unaccepted. In 1859, Shasta miners expelled the Chinese from many mining sites. By 1868, the *Republican Free Press* reported on a rousing anti-Chinese meeting resulting in a Shasta County Anti-Chinese Non-Partisan Association.

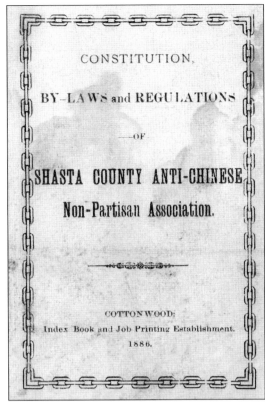

This collage is part of the Litsch collection. The photograph is of John Washington Ball, a pioneer of 1850. The piece of wedding dress and lock of hair are allegedly those of Mary Bell Washington, the mother of George Washington.

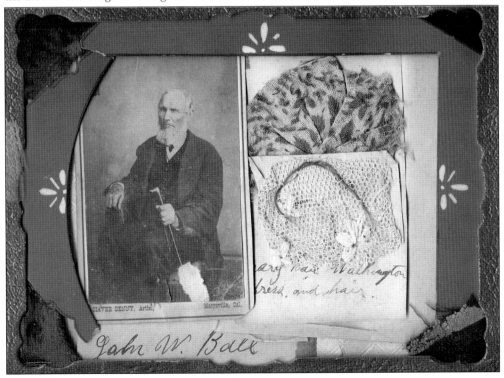

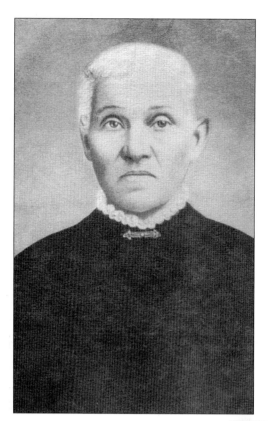

Mahala Coffey arranged for her three youngest children to be shipped via the Underground Railroad to their grandmother in Canada. The Coffey girls, Sarah and Orofino, remained in Canada to be educated there, when their father, Alvin, returned to Missouri with the intention of taking the whole family to freedom in California. The 1870 census finds them as a family in Shasta.

Alvin Aaron Coffey came to California overland on the Lassen Trail, driving a team of oxen for his master, Dr. Bassett. Arriving in Reading Springs in 1849, Coffey worked the mines for his master and other miners to earn his own freedom. Dr. Bassett returned to Missouri, took all the earnings, and sold Coffey. His new master allowed Coffey to return to California and earn his freedom a second time. Coffey also earned enough to free his wife, Mahala, and his children. The 1860 census lists Coffey, his wife, and four sons—John, Alvin, Stephen, and Charles—in Shasta.

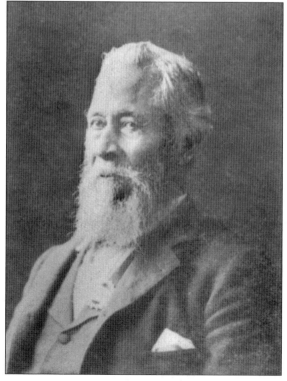

On December 30, 1865, this petition was written by parents and guardians of African American and American Indian children to establish a school for them. It was filed, acted upon, and in operation by February 1866. Dr. Pelham's daughter Sarah was the teacher, and school met first in the home of Alvin and Mahala Coffey.

To the Trustees of the Shasta School District
Gentlemen

The undersigned Parents and Guardians of colored and Indian Children hereby petition your Honorable Board of Trustees to establish a school for the benefit of the above named Children, and desire to retain Miss Nettie Reid as Teacher.

Names.		No of Children
A Grotefend	guardian of	one.
G A Pindell	" " "	one.
Alvin A. Coffey.	Parent "	five.
Edward Johnson.	" "	two.
Austin Henderson	Guardian "	two.
H. H. Henderson	" " "	one.
Elizabeth Dixon	" " "	one.
Abel Colburn.	" " "	one.

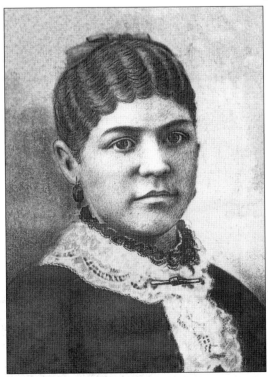

Phoebe Colburn came to California with guide and explorer James Beckworth. How Colburn attained her freedom and headed west is unknown. In Shasta, June 1854, Colburn paid Harrison Shurtleff $700 for a house, thus beginning the career of a black businesswoman, shrewd in buying and selling property and lending money. On legal documents, she was only able to leave a mark; she could neither read nor write. She died in 1875 and is buried in the Pioneer Cemetery. Colburn directed her estate should go "to her best friend of all others on earth"—Col. William Magee, who was a surveyor and miner in Shasta from 1850 to 1888.

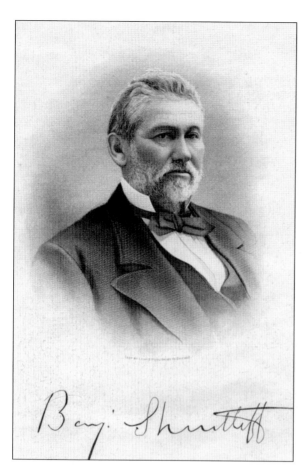

Benjamin Shurtleff, a Massachusetts native, received his medical degree from Harvard in 1848 and headed west via the Straits of Magellan in 1849. He briefly mined in Middle Creek and then began practicing medicine. In 1853, he returned home to marry Ann Griffith. He served as alcalde in 1850, state senator from 1862 to 1864, and then moved to Napa in 1874.

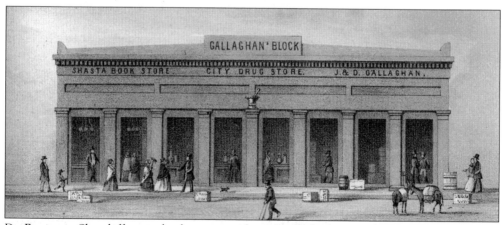

Dr. Benjamin Shurtleff opened a drugstore and mercantile business with partners A. C. Brown and Dr. J. R. Robinson in 1850 or 1851 in the Callaghan Block. In 1855, the City Drug Store became Roethe's Drug Store.

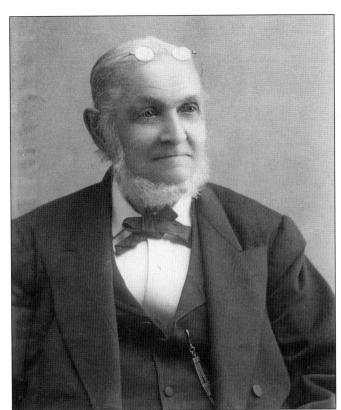

In 1853, A. L. Downer owned and operated a general merchandise store in Shasta. He established a nursery in 1858 with fruit trees and grapevines, becoming a farmer. J. W. Downer, his son, sold toys, candy, and fruit from his father's former location, shown below.

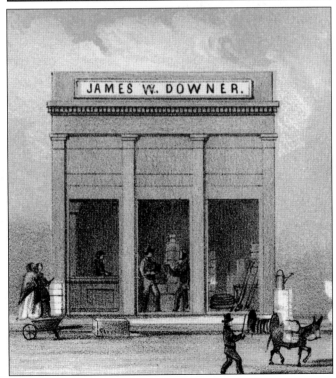

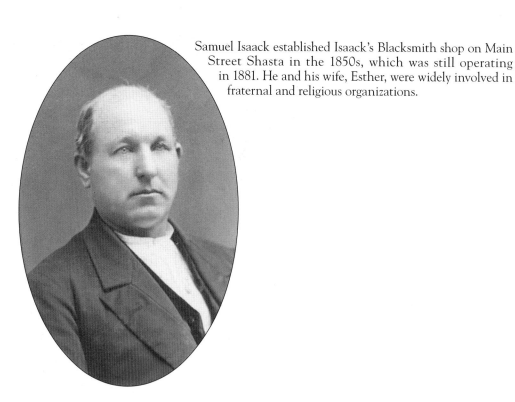

Samuel Isaack established Isaack's Blacksmith shop on Main Street Shasta in the 1850s, which was still operating in 1881. He and his wife, Esther, were widely involved in fraternal and religious organizations.

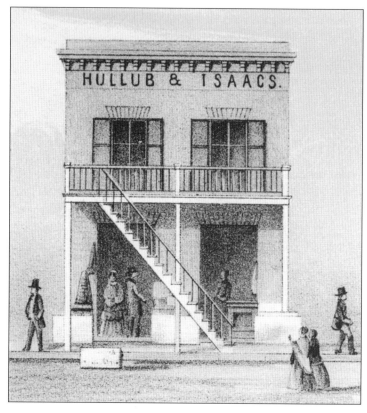

Joseph Isaacs was a member of Hullub and Isaacs, which sold everything from crockery, carpets, and playing cards to made-to-order canvas house linings, used for insulation and decoration, which were stitched on the premises. In 1854, he married Celinda Downer in Shasta.

In 1865, baker Charles Boell, pictured at right, established the U.S. Bakery, a combination bakery and saloon. From 1872 to 1875, Boell partnered with Henry Blumb to supply Shasta with a "full supply of fresh bread and cakes."

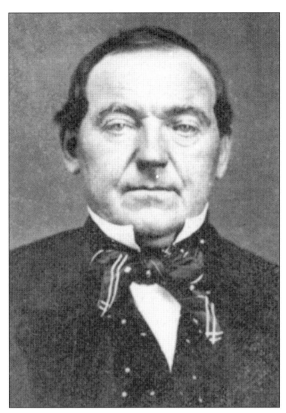

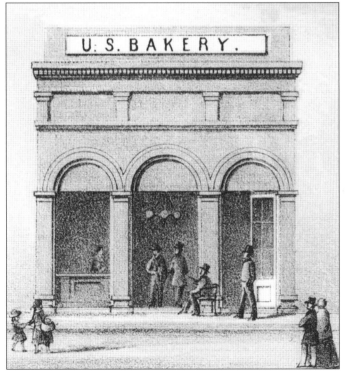

The U.S. Bakery was built on property sold by J. Henry Spatz to Boell. In 1878, a destructive fire damaged the building. Boell then bought the Garrecht saloon, running the U.S. Bakery there until his death in 1880.

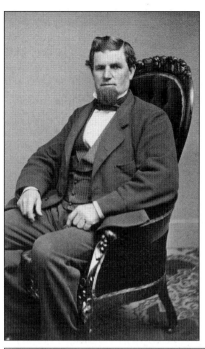

Levi Tower, gold-mining partner and later brother-in-law to Charles Camden, built the Globe Hotel on one of the parcels of property he claimed in Shasta in 1852. It was destroyed by the disastrous fire of 1853 and never rebuilt.

In 1850, James Loag was the leading mule packer operating out of Shasta. He built Loag's Block in 1855 and owned the Charter Oaks Hotel with a partner. His holdings included Loag's Horse Market and Loag's Stage Line. In 1861, the county purchased this block to remodel for the courthouse and jail.

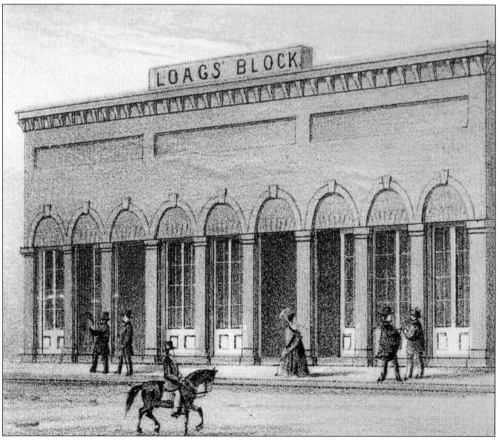

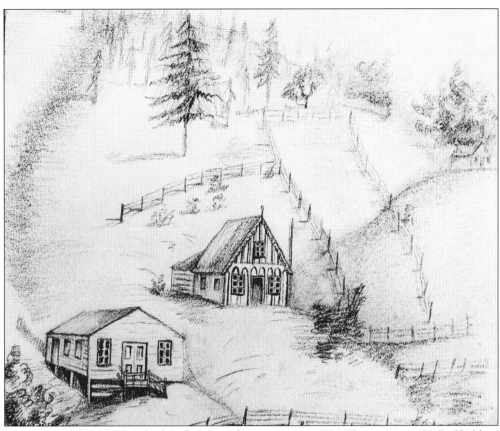

This is a sketch of the Methodist church and parsonage in 1854. The artist was H. B. Sheldon, the Methodist Episcopal minister. The improved church parsonage became the new school in Shasta with Mrs. Sheldon as teacher.

The marriage of this couple in 1852 was the second recorded wedding in Shasta County. Lucinda Bass came to Shasta by covered wagon as Mrs. James Bradley, in search of gold. Her husband was killed for his possessions while mining, leaving her a widow with a young son to support. She opened a boarding house and one of her handsome boarders was the widowed John Stephen Bass. Bass had arrived in Shasta in 1851, mining gold and operating a pack train. John Bass soon saw Lucinda as a wonderful mother for his daughter Nancy and Lucinda saw John as a good father for her son. They raised these children and others together.

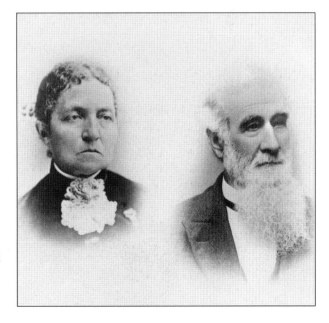

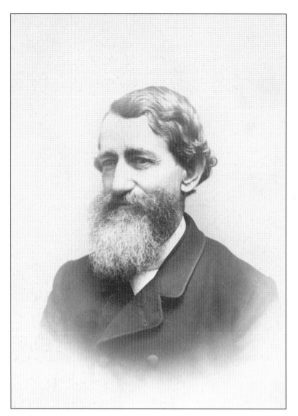

Karl August Grotefend, a German native, came overland to Shasta and, by 1849, was working diggings on Schaeffer Gulch above Middle Creek. His biggest strike of $18,000 in 1852 allowed him to purchase the St. Charles Hotel and a lot above it, where he built a cottage for his mother, Christina, and his brother Charles. In 1853, fire destroyed the hotel and Grotefend rebuilt, engaging in general merchandise. In 1854, he married Emilie Zumdahl. They raised seven children in Shasta. Only one grandchild grew to adulthood, Bessie Prehn. The Grotefends left no other descendents. Karl August did leave a diary, which definitively outlines business in Shasta from 1849 to 1853.

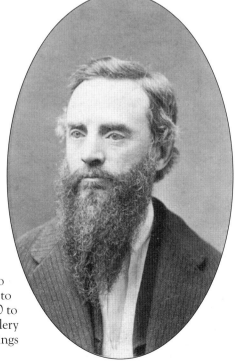

Benjamin Swasey, one of the first mining pioneers to arrive in Shasta, mined Gold Gulch, a tributary of Salt Creek, which was yielding $1,500 to the cubic yard. Settling in Lower Springs, he built a store and established a mercantile business, as well as the Swasey Hotel. Bad debts and "grub-staking" miners caused him to meet with financial reverses. He moved his family to San Francisco and worked as a photographer for 10 to 15 years, returning to Shasta in 1876 to open a gallery in the American Hotel. He lived in his Lower Springs homestead for the rest of his 92 years.

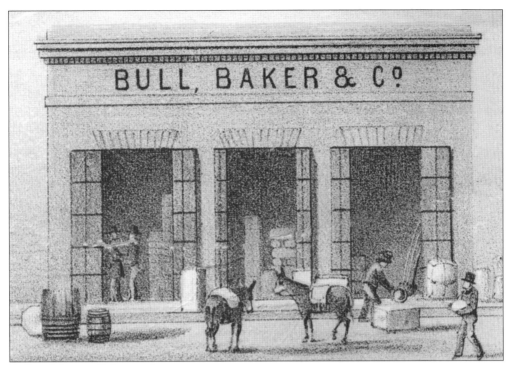

Bull and George Baker, early mining partners, created the largest wholesale business in Northern California and built the most expensive of Shasta's new "fireproof" brick buildings in 1853 at a cost of $15,000. The building sold to Advram Coleman in 1857.

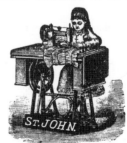
Harness maker Gunther Schroter soon made enough money in "boomtown Shasta" to send for his German sweetheart, Pauline Teuthorn. They were married in Shasta in 1859 and raised nine children here. Schroter owned harness shops in both Shasta and Redding, operated the Charter Oak Hotel, and was justice of the peace for eight years.

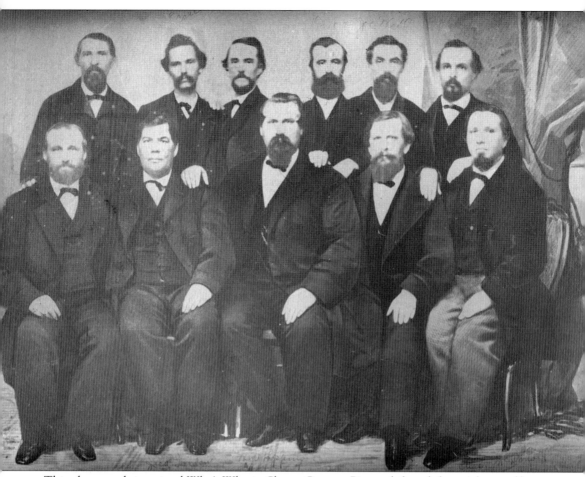

This photograph is a visual Who's Who in Shasta County. Pictured, from left to right, are (first row) unidentified; Jack Garden, county tax collector from 1864 to 1868 and county supervisor from 1881 to 1882; William Hopping, county sheriff from 1882 to 1892 and county judge from 1872 to 1880; Ed Baldwin, county road master from 1861 to 1862 and a road overseer in 1881; Charles McDonald, county clerk from 1864 to 1868; (second row) unidentified; William Carter, superintendent of schools from 1866 to 1874 and owner of *Shasta Courier* newspaper in 1869; unidentified; Dave and Joe Weil, both early Shasta vintners; and unidentified.

Three

QUEEN CITY OF THE
NORTHERN MINES

The 1850 census revealed that the Shasta Territory, which for enumeration purposes meant the area around the town of Shasta, had a population of 378 (excluding American Indians). Eight were women. The youngest were Richard Jacquett and Louisa Miller, both recorded as two years old. The oldest occupant appears to have been New Yorker Peter Brown, age 72, listed as a miner. The wealthiest resident of the area was of course, Pierson B. Reading. His occupation was listed as farmer and his wealth was estimated at $50,000. Jordan Calvert (a landlord), age 39, and John Smith (a miner), age 42, were next in wealth, with $2,500 each. A few others reported monetary assets between $200 and $2000, but the vast majority of new residents had little or no wealth to report.

Despite the apparent lack of money in the town of Shasta in the early 1850s, optimism ran high that fortunes could be made, and made quickly. A number of stores and mercantile businesses opened with the express purpose of supplying the physical needs of the miners. The key to the success of these early business ventures, of course, was the ability of their owners to secure a reliable flow of goods from Sacramento and San Francisco. To this end, a number of packet steamers such as the *Gabriel, Winter,* and the *Montgomery* cruised the Sacramento River to Colusa two or three times a week. From Colusa, freight wagons slowly worked their way up the valley on bumpy dirt roads to Shasta.

Businesses, such as O. C. Lee's California Exchange, sold wholesale and retail supplies that included groceries, provisions, liquors, hardware, crockery, clothing, and, of course, miners' tools. Lee faced competition for supplies from J. G. Doll, who, boasting large stocks of supplies, actually listed the quantities he held. His specialty was liquor, always a hot-selling commodity. He claimed to have the following: 250 10-gallon containers of superior brandy, 100 gallons of the "Best Monougahela Whisky," 50 casks of old port wine, barrels of gin and cider, and 15,000 assorted cigars. Meanwhile, T. Levi and Company informed the citizens of Shasta that their new cigar, tobacco, and stationery store (near the St. Charles Hotel) was in "constant receipt of fresh stock." Their advertisement suggested that all of their tobacco was fresh from San Francisco, and they enticed prospective customers with the following: "Ye lovers of a prime article of weed, give us a call." It is interesting to note that Doll's store sold food products that one would not normally think would be available in a 19th century boomtown located in a remote area of Northern California. Yet his store sold quantities of cheese, raisins, pickles, oysters, clams, sardines, and brandied peaches.

Stage lines played a critical role in delivering people and mail to Shasta. One of the first was the Monroe and Company Stages. The company's stage route started in Colusa and ran north through Tehama, Red Bluff, and Reading's Ranch, arriving in Shasta in 30 hours. William

McCummins, the agent living in Shasta, helped arriving passengers get the feel of the new town and prepared the stage for its turnaround to Colusa. At the Colusa end, boats were waiting to take the mail and passengers to Sacramento.

A number of hotels and boarding houses sprang up between 1850 and 1855 as a comfortable bed and good food were in high demand by miners tired of sleeping on the ground and eating whatever they could hunt or pack. Early hotels like the Globe were built hastily from crudely milled lumber. Sleeping accommodations ranged from a comfortable straw bed to a corner of the floor near the fireplace. One of the most famous and successful hotels was the St. Charles. Opening in early 1850 and serving as a gambling establishment downstairs, the St. Charles was one of the first places weary miners would visit. Come driving rain or sizzling hot summers, the hotel operated. In 1851, Karl Grotefend bought the hotel and quickly advertised that "the entire establishment has been completely revised and refitted." He realized that patrons wanted good food and tasty liquor, so he made sure "the table be provided with every staple and delicacy the market could afford. The most imposing new brick building constructed after the 1853 fire was the three-story Empire Hotel. Accommodations in the new brick hotel proved spacious but pricey, yet the Empire remained the popular choice for travelers and those with a "bit of money."

On June 14, 1853, the prosperous little boomtown suffered a huge, raging fire. All of the major hotels, homes, and other businesses, which were all made of wood and closely packed on Main Street, were consumed in the blaze. Not to be discouraged, merchants immediately set about rebuilding their establishments—determined to use brick instead of wood. Jacobson and Company, Hollub and Issacs, and Bull, Baker, and Company all spent large sums of money to construct brick buildings and then advertise the safety of their business in the *Shasta Courier*. Dr. Benjamin Shurtleff also built a new brick building for his drugstore, while leasing out part of the structure to Goldstone and Brother's Merchandising. Shurtleff's assortment of drugs and patent medicines was impressive and he often listed them in his newspaper ads. He carried the following: S. P. Townsend's Sarasaparilla, Perry Davis' Pain Killer, Wistor's Balsam of Wild Cherry, Ayer's Cherry Pectoral, Jaynes' Expectorant, and Thompson's Eye Water. Liniments were a popular item at Shurtleff's store and he sold a wide variety of brands, including Hayes' Mexican Mustang and Hunt's Nerve and Bone. The idea was to rub these liniments into your skin for soothing, fast relief of sore and inflamed areas above and below the skin. Patent medicines were very popular in Shasta during the mid-to-late 1800s and Shurtleff carried dozens of brands. A careful read of any label described a list of ailments that the pills reportedly could cure. One of the best-selling pills was Jayne's Sanative and Ague Pills. The term sanative refers to its reliable ability to cure, in a short period of time, any ailment listed. Ague was a term use to describe what miners commonly called the "fever." This usually manifested itself in the form of chills and high body temperature and was associated with malaria.

By the late 1850s, the town of Shasta appeared to be on the road to becoming the county seat of Shasta, with its population climbing near 2,500 persons and more families moving into the town. A school had been started as early as 1853 and later two other schools were formed, one at the Methodist church and the other by Fr. Raphael Rinaldi at the Catholic church. The town grew quickly, despite the rapid depletion of easily accessible placer gold, and at the start of the 1860s, just about everyone in Shasta realized that the community was going to continue to grow—for Shasta had become the "Gateway to the Northern Gold Fields."

Stage companies, such as the Coast Overland, established regular routes and transported not only passengers, but also mail and other supplies to the gold camps and towns. This 1882 timetable includes an etching by well-known artist William Keith.

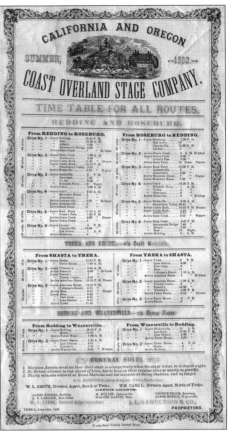

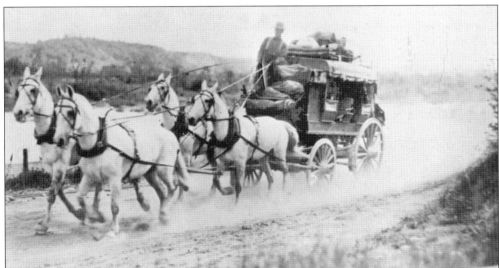

Located at the end of the freight wagon and stagecoach lines, Shasta was the commercial hub with goods and passengers transferring to and from mule trains supplying dozens of, otherwise inaccessible mining camps. Express companies were established to buy and sell enormous quantities of gold, filling a basic banking function by issuing negotiable notes for gold deposited with them.

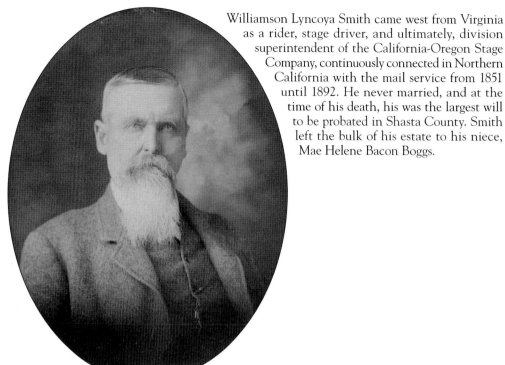

Williamson Lyncoya Smith came west from Virginia as a rider, stage driver, and ultimately, division superintendent of the California-Oregon Stage Company, continuously connected in Northern California with the mail service from 1851 until 1892. He never married, and at the time of his death, his was the largest will to be probated in Shasta County. Smith left the bulk of his estate to his niece, Mae Helene Bacon Boggs.

After the Central Pacific Railroad acquired the right-of-way, Benjamin Barnard Redding, land agent of the company, laid out the present town of Redding and so it was named for him.

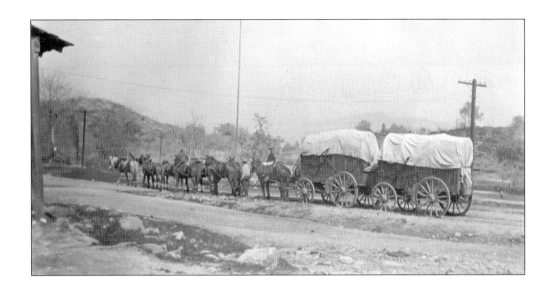

First the wagon trains, then freight wagons, pack trains, and stagecoaches all came to Shasta. An early correspondent for the *Shasta Courier* dubbed Shasta the head of "Whoa Navigation" and the name stuck. Located near the junction of three rivers and their many tributaries, Shasta was the center for commerce and transportation during its heyday. Shasta shippers and suppliers enjoyed a near monopoly in providing for the needs of miners and residents of the region. Shasta's slow decline began when the existing trails became roads pushing beyond Shasta. The above photograph was taken in the 1920s in front of the Litsch Store on Main Street in Shasta. Below, a freight train team is two miles west of Shasta in the 1870s.

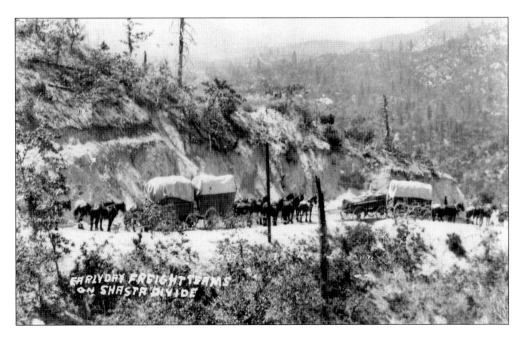

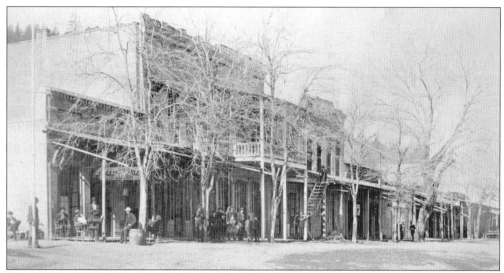

By 1849, almost 600 miners had made Shasta their home. Pioneers who came to seek their fortunes mining gold soon found that fortunes could be made in providing goods and services to the miners. Doctors and lawyers set up shop and by 1853, dozens of businesses lined Main Street. These included bathhouses, livery stables, blacksmith shops, breweries, bakeries, jewelers, and hotels. Eventually more than 50 different types of businesses served the people of Shasta.

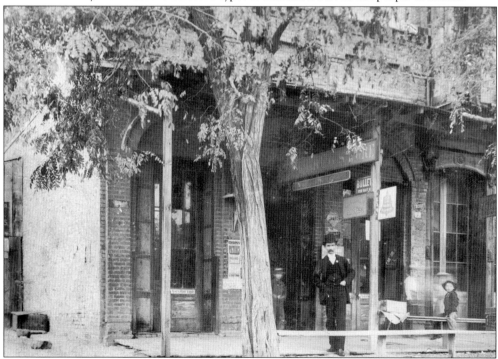

Even devastating fires couldn't kill the thriving businesses in Shasta. The first fire in the business district occurred in 1852. Another fire in June 1853 destroyed all 70 businesses in town in only 33 minutes. The rebuilding began within months, and soon businesses were proudly advertising "fireproof brick buildings." By 1855, 28 brick buildings lined Main Street, the longest row north of Sacramento. W. A. Pryor is pictured here in front of his drugstore.

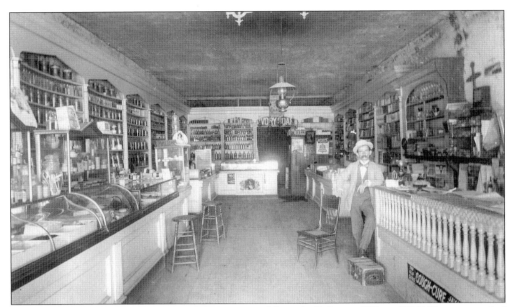

The Pryor Drug Store began as the Spatz and Litsch Saloon. When Will Pryor married Louise Litsch, the daughter of Charles and Julia Litsch, Charles gave him the location to begin a business. Will Pryor is shown here in his remodeled drugstore, which was later renamed the City Drug Store.

Without a chemist or pharmacist in house, drugstores relied on patented medicines that professed to cure a wide variety of ills.

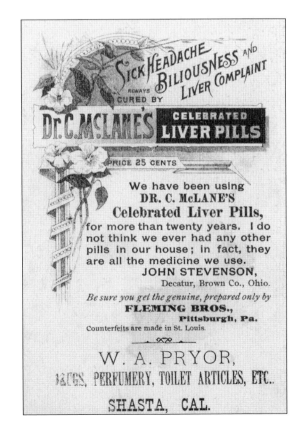

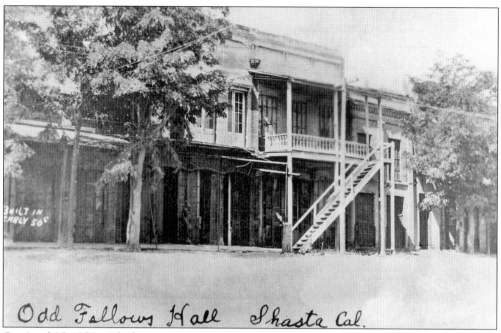

Odd Fellows Hall Shasta Cal.

On April 25, 1856, with the institution of Shasta Lodge No. 57 in Shasta, Odd Fellowship in the county began. The Odd Fellows mission is to love and care for their fraternal brothers, widows, and orphans.

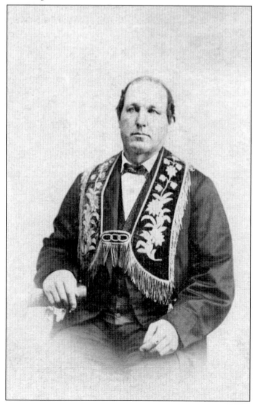

Shastan Samuel Isaacks, pictured in his ceremonial attire, served the Odd Fellows as district deputy grand master. In 1871, he and his wife, Esther, instituted the Millville Rebekah Lodge.

Fred Buck was a shoemaker in Shasta and an active Mason, well reflected in this photograph. The sash and sword are in a collection at the Masonic Lodge in Shasta.

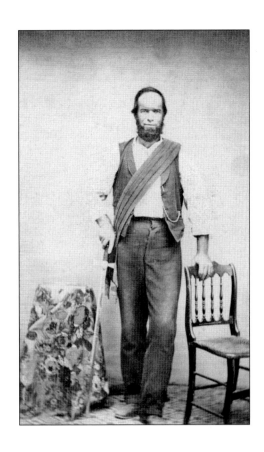

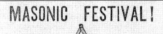

MASONIC FESTIVAL!

St. John's Day!

Wednesday, June 24th, 1868.

THE MASONIC FRATERNITY

Of Shasta and vicinity will celebrate the coming Anniversary of St. John the Baptist by a

PROCESSION AND EXERCISES

At the Church, in the forenoon, and a

GRAND BALL

AT NIGHT.

Members of the Fraternity will assemble promptly at Masonic Hall, at 10 o'clock A. M.

The Exercises at the Church will take place at about eleven o'clock, and the

Public are cordially invited to attend.

The Dinner to the Fraternity will take place at the Charter Oak Building precisely at 2 o'clock P. M.

Persons arriving in Shasta, and unable to procure accommodations, will apply to either of the following

COMMITTEE OF RECEPTION:

G. I. TAGGART.   C. C. BUSH.
G. C. SCHROTER,   J. N. CHAPPELL.
J. W. GARDEN.

The Ball at night will take place at Armory Hall, to which the public are respectfully invited.

TICKETS $5 00

By order Committee of Arrangements.   je

The grand balls and celebrations held by the Masons were social events of note. This particular event also celebrated Charter Day, the day the Masonic Lodge took possession of their charter in 1848.

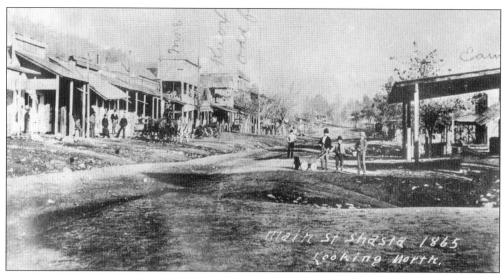

By 1852, Shasta had its own newspaper, the *Shasta Courier*. In the mid-1850s, the town's population of over 2,500 supported a variety of businesses from saloons to bookstores to several doctors and lawyers. At the time, "This was the shopping mall of the Northern California."

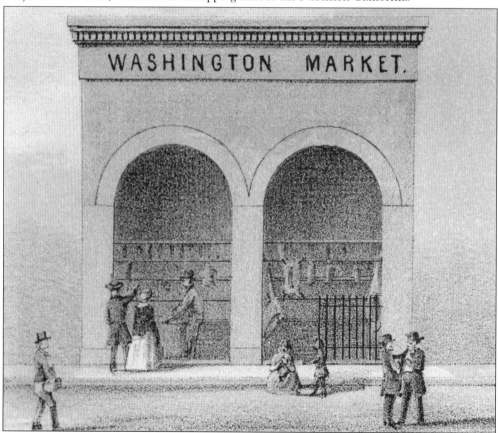

In 1853, Klotz's Washington Meat Market was owned by John and Rudolph Klotz. Their brothers Dan and Fred were employees.

Horace Wright was one of Shasta's butchers, with extended family in the area. Cattle raised in Woodland, California—140 miles south of Shasta—were driven live to the town to be butchered.

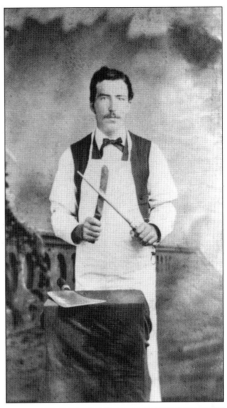

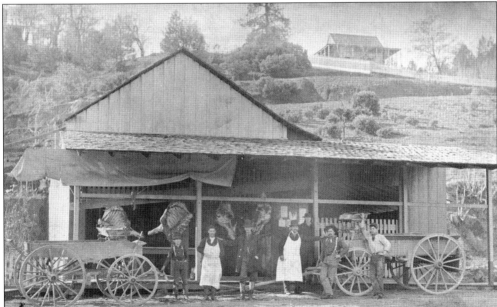

Butchers Peter Hoff and Harmon Prackle, in their signature white butchers' aprons, pose in front of Huff's Butcher shop, which began doing business as City Meat Market. Prackle bought the business in 1881. For refrigeration, the hillside was carved out in the back of the store, supported with brick, and cooled with blocks of ice brought down from Shasta Bally.

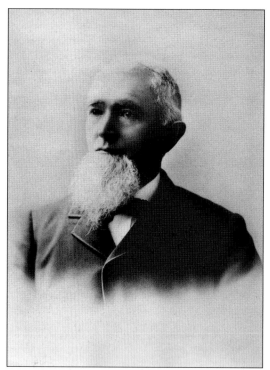

Frank Litsch joined his brother Charles in Shasta in 1853, as did many Germans fleeing the revolutions, heavy taxation, and conscription in their native land. Litsch tried mining and bartending until he founded the Litsch Store. This business enjoyed 86 years of operation. His marriage to Caroline Sheure produced three daughters and a son, Joseph, who died suddenly in 1890.

This 1880s interior photograph of the Litsch Store in Shasta was typical for the business buildings in town. They were long and narrow, usually no more than 24 feet, as the width was taxed by the county.

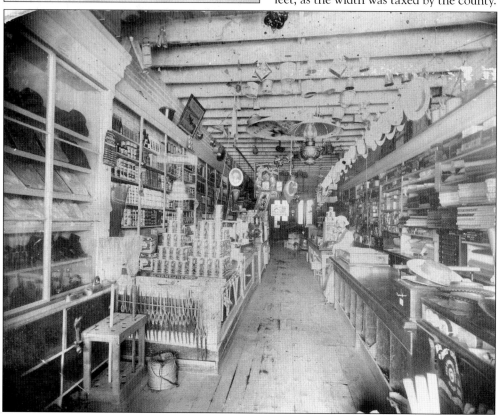

Charles Litsch emigrated from Baden, Germany, arriving in Shasta in 1851. He trained as a butcher, baker, and brewmeister. He owned successively the Spatz and Litsch Bakery and Saloon and the Behrle and Litsch Washington Brewery. He married Julia Behrle, 16 years his junior. Four daughters and a son were born to them in Shasta. In 1884, Litsch died from a fall in the brewery.

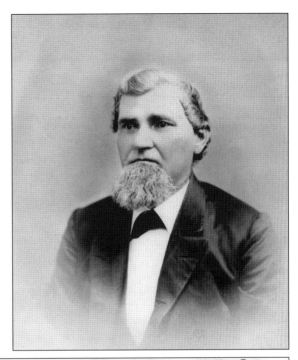

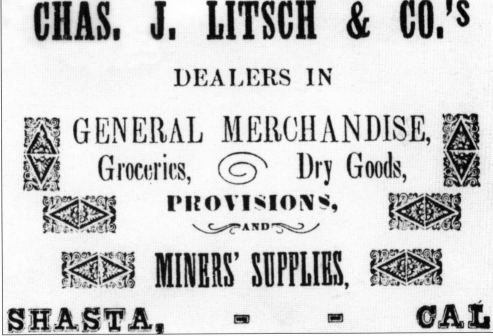

CHAS. J. LITSCH & CO.'S

DEALERS IN

GENERAL MERCHANDISE,
Groceries,   Dry Goods,
PROVISIONS,
AND

MINERS' SUPPLIES,

SHASTA,   —   —   CAL

In 1895, Charles Joseph Litsch and his mother, Julia Behrle Litsch, purchased the Litsch Store from his aunt and uncle. In 1928, Charles Joseph became the sole owner upon his mother's death. As Shasta decayed, the store became more a museum and post office and the stage stopover became a gas station. Charles Joseph died in 1938, leaving the store to his son Charles Robert. Charles Robert "Bob" Litsch ran the store/museum until 1960, when he sold all to the state to add to Shasta State Historic Park.

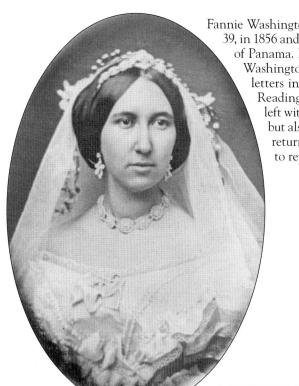

Fannie Washington Reading, 25, married P. B. Reading, 39, in 1856 and returned to California over the Isthmus of Panama. Rancho life was busy and far from the Washington social scene she grew up in, but her letters indicate she enjoyed her new life. Upon Reading's death in 1868, not only was Fannie left with the entire responsibility of the ranch, but also five children under the age of 11. She returned east when the ranch had to be sold to repay a debt.

Jeanette (Nellie) Reading was an infant when her mother, Reading's first wife, died in 1842. She joined the family at Rancho Buena Ventura in 1860 as a teenager, having been cared for by relatives and educated in New Orleans. Jeannette remained in California and married Capt. Robert Simson.

The twins, Richard Washington Reading (left) and Robert Lee Reading (right), were born in 1863 and only five when their father died. Richard became a mining engineer, serving in France as a major in the Corps of Army Engineers during World War I. He lived in Shasta County on his inherited third of the Washington section of Rancho Buena Ventura. Robert became an elected county surveyor in Shasta County.

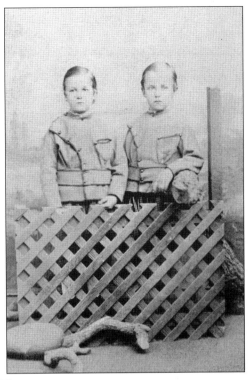

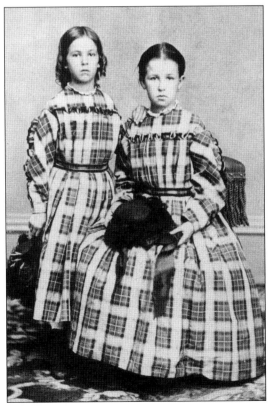

Neither Alice Washington Reading (left) nor Anna Matilda Reading married. Alice studied at the Corcoran School of Art, specializing in portraiture. Alice painted Judge Edward Sweeny's portrait that hangs in the renovated courtroom at the Courthouse Museum in Shasta State Historic Park and also that of John Bidwell that hangs in the hall of Bidwell Mansion in Chico. Anna wrote under the nom-de-plume, Dorsey Barton, and for 20 years, was an expert on classification of electrical engineering data in the Scientific Library of the Patent Office in Washington. She met a tragic death in 1906, a fatality in a train wreck.

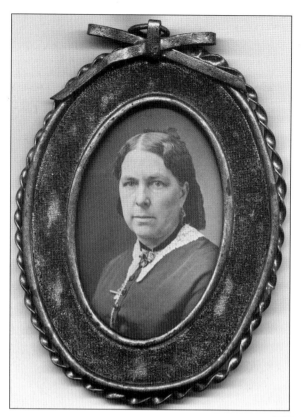

Frances Blocksum Sprague, beloved wife and mother, crossed the Isthmus of Panama with her husband, R. T. Sprague, and her children, Anna and Arthur, to make her home in Shasta. Frances brought to Shasta a genteel tradition, so lacking in the pioneer gold-rush town. Mrs. Sprague served the community by joining many of the town's volunteer committees and helping to organize others. An infant daughter Ella is buried in the Shasta Union Cemetery. Another daughter, Frances Royal Sprague, born in 1864 in Shasta, never married, but became a practicing physician in San Francisco.

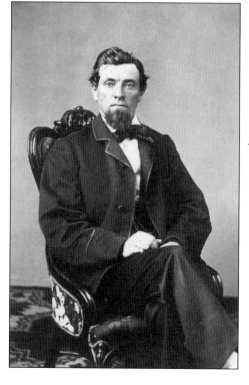

The 1860 census indicates Charles McDonald was a 32-year-old expressman from Scotland. In Shasta, McDonald established McDonald's Saloon, where leaders of the community gathered for evening nightcaps and discussion. McDonald was one of those leaders, serving as county clerk. Shasta's McDonald Alley is named for him.

This 1868 certificate validates that Lorenz Garrecht and Amelia Prehn were joined in marriage by G. R. Knox, justice of the peace, in compliance with the law according to Charles McDonald, county clerk. By convention, early legal documents in Shasta were handwritten. The county seal and stamp provided authenticity.

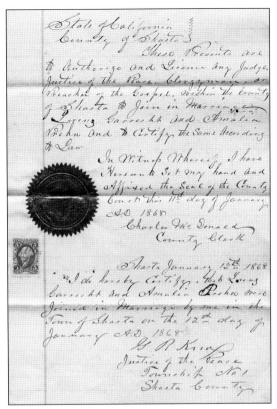

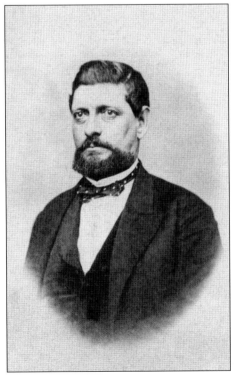

George R. Knox was a 38-year-old miner from New York, according to the 1860 census. In 1853, he came to mine, settling in the Whisky Creek area. By 1862, he had moved to Shasta, opening a saloon, billiard parlor, and later, adding a reading room advertising "newspapers and periodicals from nearly every state in the Union with the best wines, liquors and cigars at the bar."

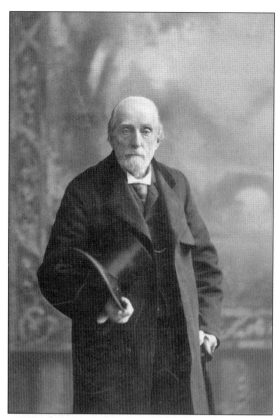

Dr. James E. Pelham advertised himself as a physician, surgeon, and accoucheur (obstetrician). In 1855, Pelham was first to be appointed as hospital physician at the county hospital in Shasta. His Main Street office was two doors above Bentley's Livery Stable. Pelham also served on the first board of trustees for Shasta Township with R. T. Sprague and Harrison Shurtleff. His daughter Sarah, a teacher, married Solomon Brastow, a pioneer stage driver and Wells Fargo agent.

Wells Fargo and Company Express was established in 1852 to buy, sell, and transport the miners' gold, and to function as a bank. The company's checks and receipts were "as good as gold" and their agents were scrupulously honest. Chosen from among Shasta's most reputable businessmen to be agents were Mr. Hopping and Mr. Dobrowsky.

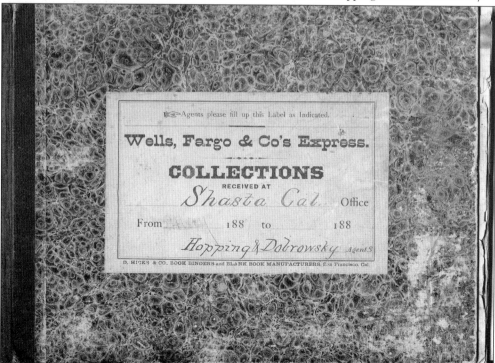

Brothers Adolph and Ernest Dobrowsky were Argonauts of 1849. Adolph was a jeweler and watchmaker, and Ernest a jeweler and gunsmith, both with separate businesses. Adolph opened his first store in Coloma in 1851 and in Shasta in 1854. His notable garden in Shasta was described as a "prim, old-fashioned one with flowers and shrubs of rare and choice varieties." The man himself was reportedly "generous and hospitable to visitors with the eye and hand of an artist and a great love of nature."

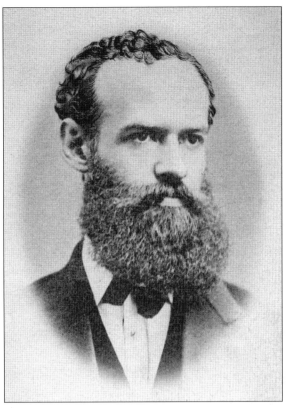

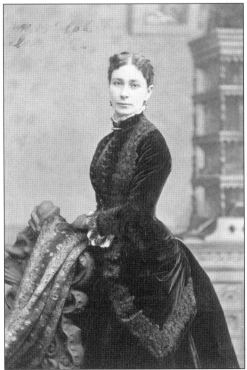

Nellie Reid Dobrowsky came to Shasta in 1854, teaching at the segregated school on Second Street. By 1872, pupils were integrated into a new brick school. Mrs. Dobrowsky reported these interesting school facts: teachers earned $35 a month, a school term was three months, and the older Mullen boys were asked to bring their guns to school to protect their classmates from American Indians.

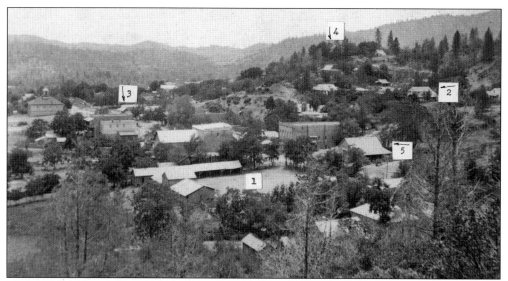

This numbered, aerial view of Shasta shows 1) the Empire Hotel corral and wagon yard, 2) the Bystle home, allegedly the first wood-frame home in 1850 Shasta, 3) the Litsch Store, 4) the Shurtleff Home, and 5) Isaack's Blacksmith shop.

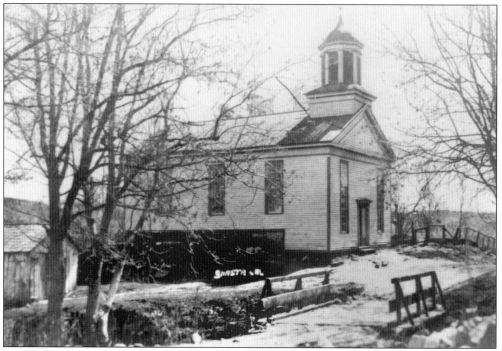

The bell tower in Shasta's Methodist church housed a silver bell given by Col. William Magee and made from silver taken from his Iron Mountain mine. George Albro recalled that when he rang the bell for deaths in Shasta, he also recorded their names in the tower. The church burned in 1927. The first minister of the Methodist Episcopal church in 1852 was Rev. John Hill, "a muscular Christian," who one day when he was preaching outdoors was impeded by a gambler from continuing. Hill pitched the man bodily over the railing of the sidewalk into the street. So much for forbearance!

Emanuel Lewin emigrated from Bohemia. In 1853, he was associated with the firm Lewin and Schwartz, jewelers and watchmakers in Shasta. In 1861, E. Lewin and Company advertised as "assayers of gold and ore offering San Francisco rates." Lewin was trustee for the Hebrew Congregation of Shasta County and father of Benno, Alex, and Anna.

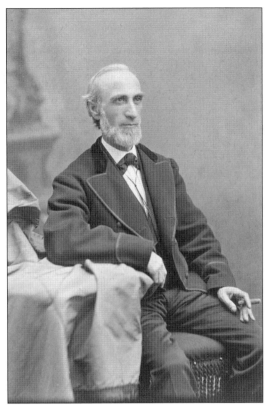

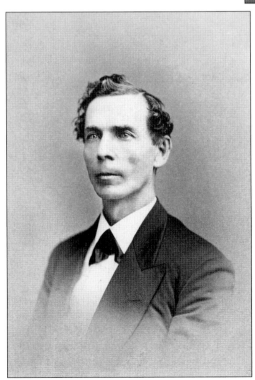

Ferdinand Baehr was associated with Lewin as an assayer, purchasing gold dust from miners. In San Francisco, Baehr met and married a widow with four children, all of whom he brought home to Shasta. One of those children was Ida Matilda, who later became the wife of C. C. Bush.

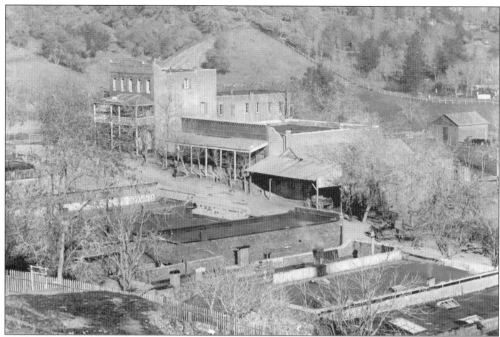

According to the May 29, 1879, *Shasta Courier,* "from a reporter of the People's Cause, who returned this morning from a ramble up north, we learn that Shasta is fast recovering from the effects of the fire of last July. New buildings are being erected, old ones being repaired and painted and the town resuming a lively appearance generally. Several new quartz ledges are being opened with encouraging prospects near town and others that have been idle for years are again being worked. That the citizens feel assured of lively times in the near bye and bye is evincible by the preparations they are making for a grand celebration of the coming 4th of July, nearly $1,000 being already subscribed toward it." Seen here are views of Shasta in the 1870s.

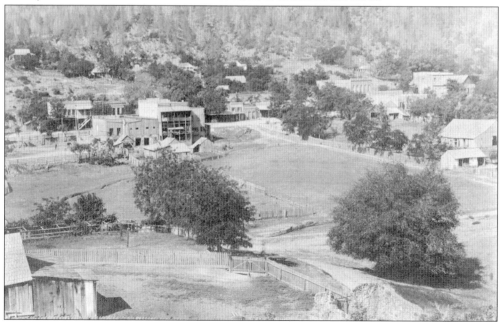

William Stephen (W. S.) Wills arrived in Shasta from Maine in the 1850s and made a fortune in produce, bricks, and real estate sales. He constructed a two-story brick building between the Odd Fellow's Hall and Tomlinson and Wood as rental property. Two of his three daughters were born in Shasta. In 1878, he returned to Maine, dying there.

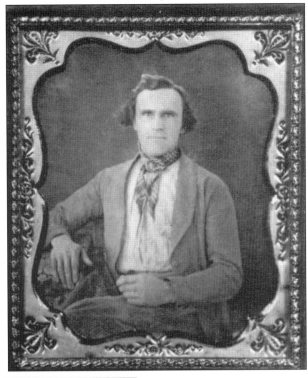

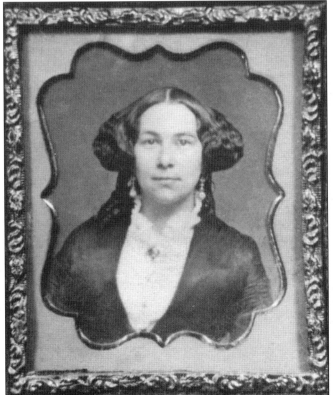

Esther Jane Wills joined her husband, W. S., traveling from Maine to Shasta with their daughter Ellen to live on 40 acres east of Shasta. She recalls "over a trail near the house, files of scantily clad Indians used to pass, curious, but friendly." Esther and her two daughters Ida and Essie, both born in Shasta, returned with W. S. Wills to Maine in 1878.

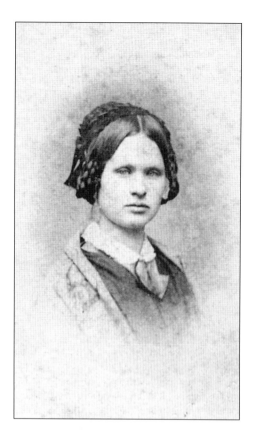

Emily Marshal Swasey came west with daughter Emily to join her husband, Ben, is his mercantile and hotel operation at Lower Springs. She died in San Francisco in the 1868 smallpox epidemic.

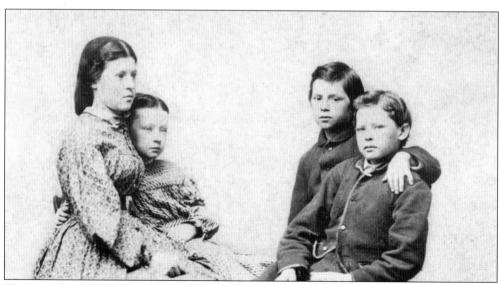

These are the children of Benjamin and Emily Swasey. Emily was born in New Hampshire; Alice, Frank, and Fred in Shasta. All became Shasta County residents.

Four

FACES IN THE CROWD

Without a doubt, single, young men dominated the population of early Shasta. Bent on striking it rich, these wide-eyed, courageous pioneers crossed the continent by wagon train or sailed around the Horn to get to California. Many of them had tried their luck placer mining in the Sierra Nevada gold fields before moving up to the "northern reaches." Early census reports noted that a goodly number of these first residents of the "Queen City" had come directly from Europe. England, Ireland, and Germany appear to have been the main countries of origin of these emigrants. It is not clear from the 1850 census if any blacks were among the earliest residents of Shasta, but by 1853 a town census reported "48 Male Negros, 3 Females."

At first, the main "community" holding the miners together was the desire for survival and the opportunity to swap gold-prospecting stories. Law and order were important and the miners actively took part in regular town meetings that discussed establishing a court of sessions, clearing and maintaining roads, and the formulation of regulations. William B. Harrison, the first judge of the court of sessions, tried a number of important court cases that put Shasta on track as a law-abiding community. Ironically the community "events" that brought out the biggest crowds were murder trials. One example was the 1855 trial and execution of Alexander Higgins, who was found guilty of killing his partner with an axe. The Higgins hanging brought out "the entire town" according to the sheriff and a "goodly number of people not residing in Shasta."

As early as April 1852, community events such as the spring races helped to bring the community of Shasta together. Sponsored by T. J. Stump, the races were held in a field two miles from the town. Stump put together a complete program of events, which included not only horse racing, but also mule and jackass races, a cockfight, and a demonstration of gymnastic exercises. One miner, known as "Old Dutch," challenged all comers to a footrace for "a sum anywhere between $10 and $100."

In addition to the large number of miners living in Shasta, numerous professionals resided in the town and provided their services. Some of the earliest lawyers in Shasta included: William Daingerfield, with an office in the rear of the St. Charles Hotel; Robert Trevis; and W. R. Harrison, with an office at the Shasta Hotel. William Robinson, another attorney in Shasta, ran his business from the Shasta Hotel also and advertised that he was the "Quartz Recorder for Shasta County." Several physicians practiced medicine from the earliest days of the boomtown and some of the more successful doctors included Benjamin Shurtleff and Henry Bates.

Benjamin Shurtleff, easily one of the most recognizable citizens of Shasta, maintained an excellent reputation as an able and honest man. In 1850, fellow miners elected him alcalde (Mexican mayor), or judge. Of course, his talents in the medical field were also noticed and his medical practice helped many early Shasta residents. In addition, he invested commercially and owned several successful businesses, such as his drugstore.

Royal T. Sprague, a prominent attorney, notified the citizens of Shasta in March 1853 that even though he had been absent from the area for months, he was now ready to devote his full attention to the legal needs of the town. He had been one of the original forty-niners, coming from a successful situation in Ohio. Sprague's hard work in community building, including his efforts to start the first public school in the area, helped to get him elected to the state Senate and later a stint on the California Supreme Court.

Some faces in the crowd disappeared almost as quickly as they arrived in Shasta. Due to the nature of gold mining, prospectors would come into town, stay for a few days, buy the supplies they needed, and then head out into the mountains. Every so often, they would vanish for weeks or months at a time. Sometimes family members would place ads in the *Shasta Courier* newspaper hoping that a townsperson might have seen the missing individual. One way to have your face remembered was to have it photographed and there was a photographer in Shasta from the earliest years of the 1850s. J. Ruth described himself as a daguerreotype artist and he set up business in the St. Charles Hotel. This early method of photography involved chemically producing the image on a plate of metal or glass. Ruth produced his images in many different sizes, including tiny photographs that could be placed in lockets, pins, rings, watches, and seals. He advertised that "persons wishing to secure good life-like pictures will please call soon—likenesses taken in all kinds of weather and satisfaction is guaranteed."

A large number of Chinese miners worked and lived in and around the town of Shasta. Population estimates of local Chinese ranged from a low of "a hundred or so" to over 500 persons. For the most part, they worked the less desirable claims or reworked old claim sites. The Lower Springs section of Shasta, a popular location for newly arrived immigrants, became known as "Hong Kong." By 1854, white miners felt threatened by the increasing number of Chinese arriving and called several town meetings to discuss what to do with the "Chinamen." Claiming that the Chinese have "utterly overspread the land and become a nuisance too intolerable," one group of white miners suggested an actual invasion: "menial millions are flocking to our shores," and "in a short period of time" they will control most of the state. For many of the miners, the answer to the Chinese problem was two-fold—first they must "unite in keeping them from the mines" and second, if necessary, "drive them entirely out of the country."

Few women lived in town during the earliest years of Shasta, but by 1853 there were over 200 women in town. The first reported woman in the tiny town was reported to be an unnamed female "imported" by the owners of the Trinity Hotel to "keep and manage the house." As more women arrived to live in town, they formed clubs or associations to help with civic development and to actively aid and support each other. Frances Sprague arrived in Shasta in the mid-1850s and, with her husband and Isaac Roop, immediately set out to establish a school and to improve community participation. In 1859, she helped to establish the Mount Vernon Ladies Association, that held regular social events. One interesting account is of Phoebe Colburn, a black woman and former slave, who owned a home originally built by Harrison Shurtleff. Records show that she paid a substantial amount of money ($700) for the house in 1854, yet no one is sure where she obtained the funds.

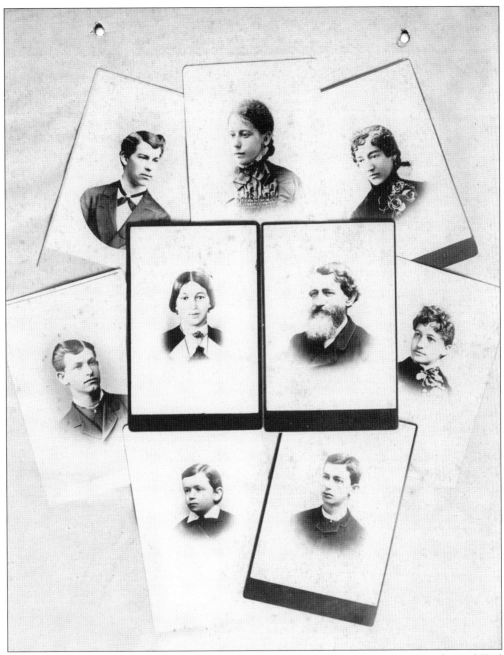

This early photographic collage is of the pioneer Grotefends. In the center are Emelia and Karl August Grotefend. Their children and Karl's youngest brother appear surrounding them.

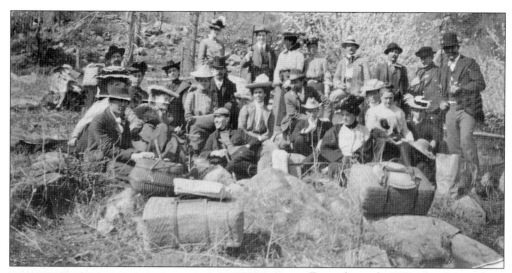

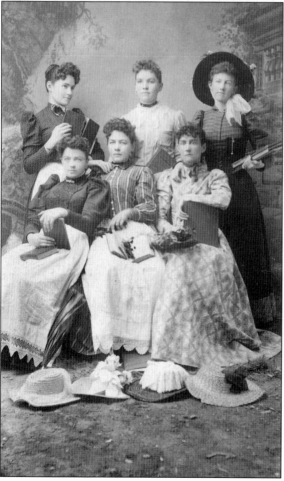

From the early 1850s, residents of Shasta could choose from the many balls and theatrical and literary events available in the town's hotels and meeting places. Holidays like the Fourth of July and New Year's Day were celebrated in style. Families picnicked by the streams and in meadows. Those who wanted to keep up with their reading and current events had two bookstores and a newspaper to keep them informed. More active entertainment could be found in the bowling alley, billiards parlor, or roller skating rink located in the Charter Oak Hotel.

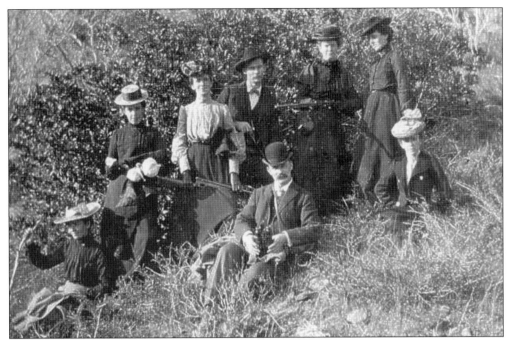

Pictured here are the ladies of the Winchester Rifle Club. Visit the Courthouse Museum to view pocket pistols (also known as muff guns because they were concealed in hand muffs) and buggy rifles.

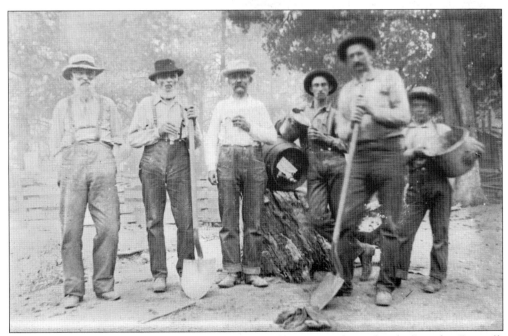

Putting out the forest fire near the Old Slaughterhouse are Shasta locals Grandpa Boswell, E. F. Crocker, and Nibs Schroter.

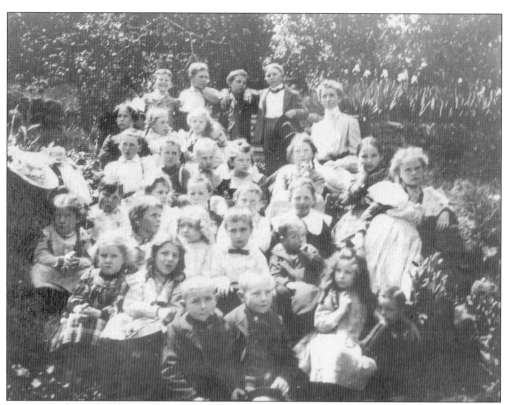

This photograph of a group of children was taken in front of their Sunday school in Shasta in the 1880s.

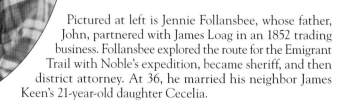

Pictured at left is Jennie Follansbee, whose father, John, partnered with James Loag in an 1852 trading business. Follansbee explored the route for the Emigrant Trail with Noble's expedition, became sheriff, and then district attorney. At 36, he married his neighbor James Keen's 21-year-old daughter Cecelia.

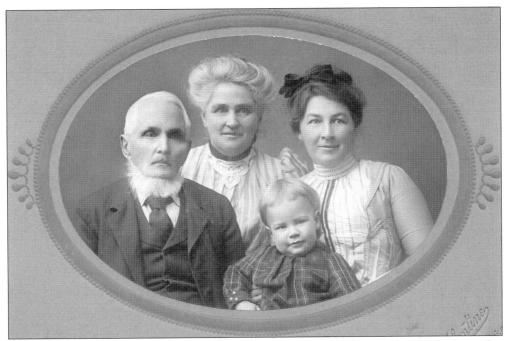

Four generations of Shastans, seen in this photograph from left to right, are Everett French Crocker (first generation), his daughter Eunice Francis Crocker Blair (second generation), her daughter Martha Blair Lamus (third generation), and her son Blair Barnard Lamus (fourth generation).

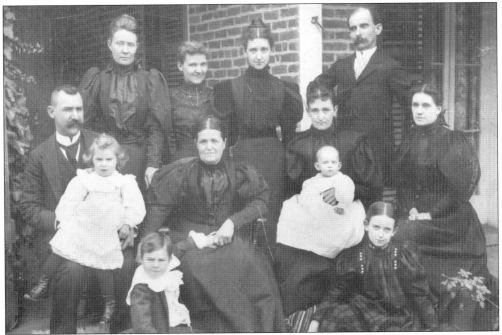

This photograph of the Litsch family was taken in 1897. Pictured, from left to right, are (first row) Charles Robert Litsch and Ellie Maude Pryor; (second row) Charles J. Litsch, Hilda Litsch, Julia Behrle Litsch, and Ethel Pryor Beers; (third row) Varena Miles Litsch, Fannie Litsch, May Litsch Duffy, and William A. Pryor. The two young children sitting on laps are not identified.

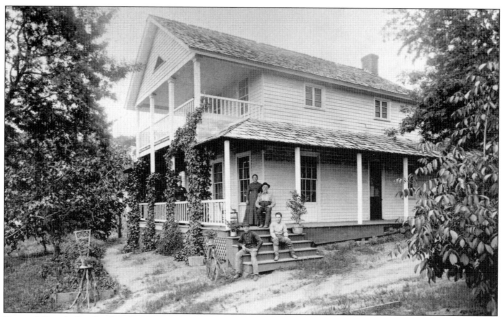

Daniel Bystle built this home in the 1850s and soon established himself in the carpentry and undertaking business in Shasta. In 1866, Bystle, a widower, married a widow, Amelia Heffelfinger, raising her two children here.

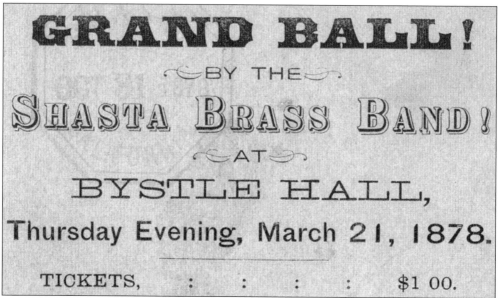

The Grand Ball was an entertainment for ladies and gentlemen with carefully proscribed rules of etiquette and dress. Shasta was not only a center for business, but also a place where, in the early 1850s, residents could choose from the many balls, theatrical, and literary events that were available in hotels and meeting places.

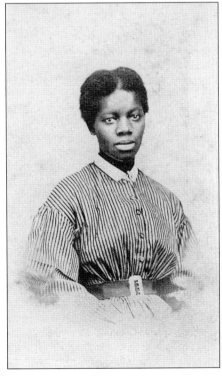

The photograph album was as important a parlor feature as the family Bible, heralding the popular social practice of exchanging pictures with friends and relatives. Both of these images were taken from just such an album. The above photograph is of Mrs. Charles Fordham, and the image below comes from an album inscribed "From Chas. Lee Williams to Anna Bass Baird 1895." The back of the photograph identifies the woman as "Clara Twine, Came to Cal. with Mr. and Mrs. Williams. Saw Mill Flat. Shasta Co. Cal." Both dress styles appear to be from the 1860s.

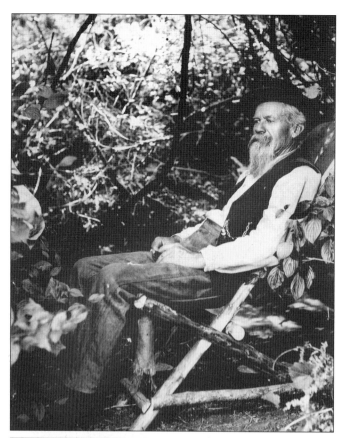

Lorenz Garrecht, another member of Shasta's German group, arrived in 1852 and partnered with Peter Hoff in a butcher shop. In 1868, Lorenz Garrecht married Amelia Prehn, purchasing the house below for $225 in gold coin.

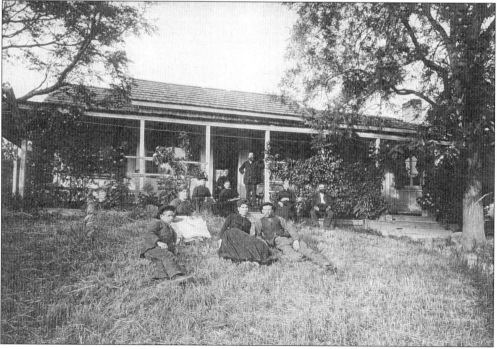

Dr. John Milton Briceland was a Shasta physician and surgeon with offices located beside the U.S. Land Office in Shasta. He presided at the hangings of Baker and Crouch, certifying their death.

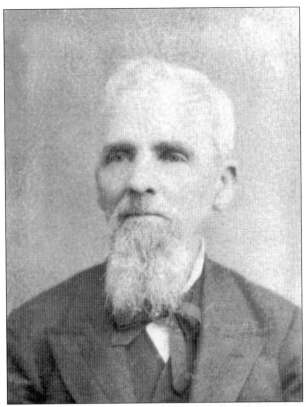

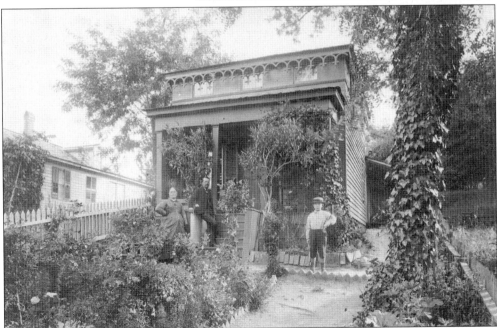

The Brunning House was built entirely of packing crates used to ship merchandise to Shasta. Wooden lace eaves camouflage the patchwork origin. Carpenter Eugene Crowell built the house, sold it to W. L. Carter, who sold it to Henry Brunning, pictured with his wife and son Eddie.

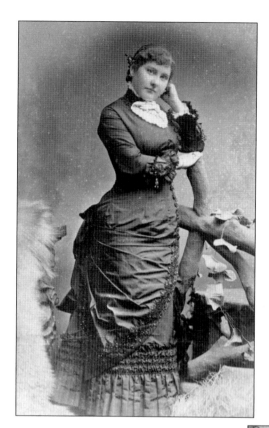

Mae Helene Bacon, 17 years old, took the stage to boarding school in Yreka with her Shasta friends. This is her graduation photograph in 1880.

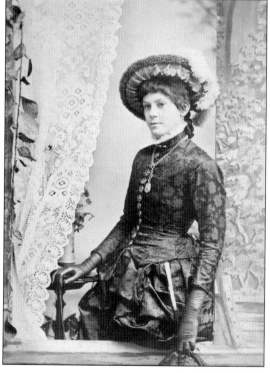

Miss Jennie Bailey, the "prettiest girl in Shasta County," never married. She was the daughter of Joseph and Hester Bailey, who came west on the Bailey-McMurphy train in 1864. Jennie was born at a stopping place called Four Mile House, only four miles from Shasta.

On May 27, 1883, William Miller Crum of Igo and Cynthia Florella Wright of Shasta were married by Rev. C. W. Darling in the Methodist church in Shasta. They raised seven sons and seven daughters in Shasta and both are buried in the Masonic cemetery.

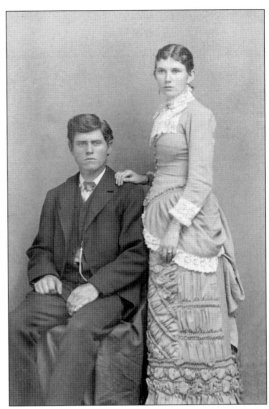

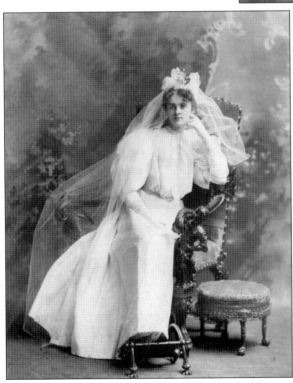

Dressed and photographed as a Victorian woman would be, this lovely bride is intriguingly identified only as Cozy Dunn.

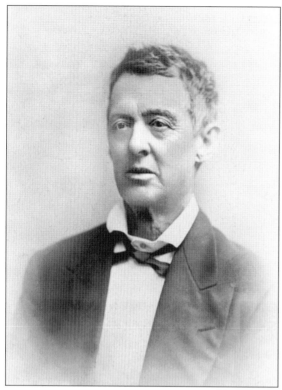

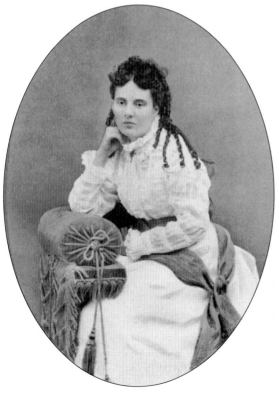

Jonathan and Alice Gage came west to join her brother Benjamin Swasey, leaving their three children with New England relatives. Their humorous letters home offer a perspective on life in Shasta. Jonathan drew a picture of their new log home, only 18 by 30 feet, with cloth partitions and a hard dirt floor, and pronounced it "was the house that Jack built." Alice wrote of sitting at the kitchen table with "three loaded pistoles on the table to shute rats as big as a decent size kitten" and hiding a precious bag of their gold in a flour barrel, only to surprise a would-be burglar with the sight of one of her immense pistoles aimed straight at him.

Dr. Louis Wellendorf arrived in Shasta in 1851, establishing a drugstore with his nephew and partner, Rudolph Saeltzer, a German chemist. In 1859, Wellendorf became a naturalized citizen.

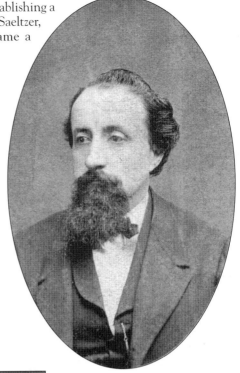

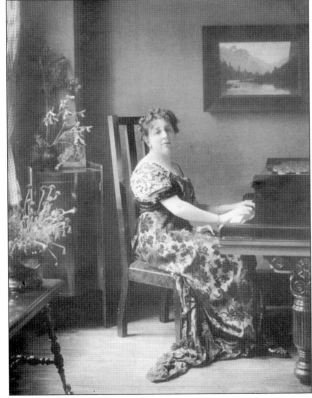

Adaline Maude Wellendorf, Dr. Wellendorf's daughter by his first marriage, was born in Shasta and became a concert pianist. Her Shasta teacher was her stepmother, Mildred Bacon Bartlett.

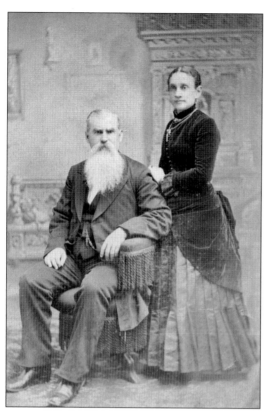

In 1851, Chauncey Carroll Bush worked in Shasta as a mule packer and unsuccessful gold miner. Later he served as county judge in 1861 and was admitted to the bar in 1867. In 1865, he married Ida Schroeder. With the arrival of the railroad, he moved his family to Redding.

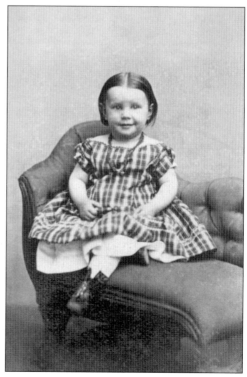

C. C. and Ida Bush had five children. Eda (at right) and her brother Carroll were born in Shasta; her brothers George and Harry and little sister Jennie in Redding.

Nellie Voluntine Wood, of Tomlinson and Wood Hardware in Shasta, was educated at Napa Collegiate Institute, which became University of the Pacific in Stockton. She married a classmate, Charles Shurtleff, who rose to be an associate justice of the Supreme Court of California. Both were born and raised in Shasta.

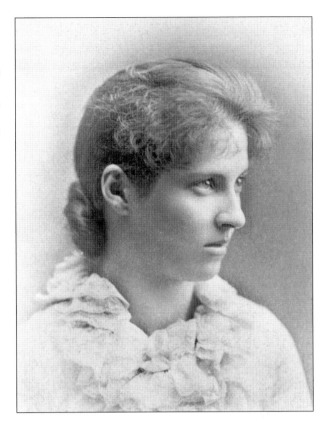

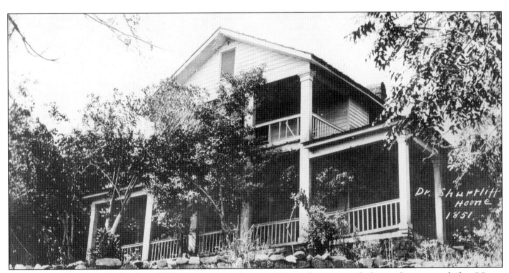

The Shurtleff House, pictured here, was built in 1851 with materials brought around the Horn from Maine. When the Masonic Lodge lost their meeting hall to fire in 1853, they met at the Shurtleff's house. It was sold to John Schultz in 1874, W. L. Carter in 1877, and Albert McConnell in 1884. When it burned in 1967, it had been continuously occupied for 120 years.

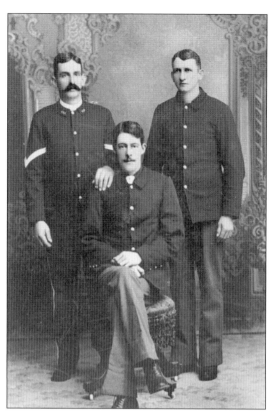

The "good old Shasta boys" pictured here are Gunther Frederick and Arthur Schroter (standing), sons of Shasta's harness maker, and Fred Schuler, possibly George Frederick Schuler's son.

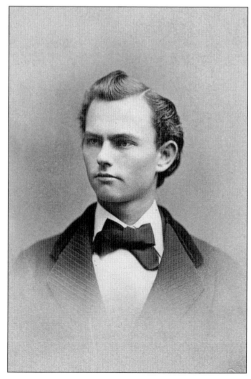

This is one of Benjamin Shurtleff's three sons—George C. (1854), Charles A. (1857), or Benjamin E. (1867)—all born in Shasta.

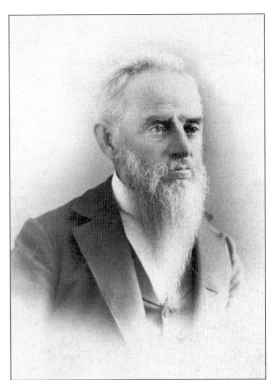

In 1876, Benjamin Swasey and his second wife, Nellie Dalton Swasey, returned to Shasta. They had two sons, George and Benjamin. Swasey devoted himself to photography, advertising that he would take photographs from "life size down," and his fine orchards, indulging in a passion for propagating superior fruit trees.

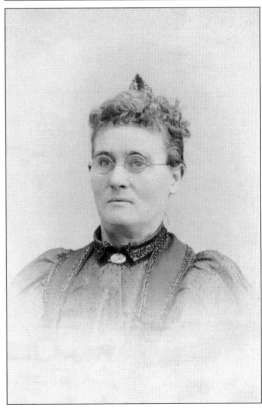

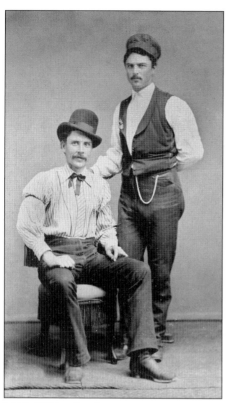

Brothers Frank (standing) and Fred (seated) Swasey were born and lived as adults in Shasta County. Frank became owner and publisher of the *Redding Free Press* in 1879, and Fred Park Swasey became a photographer like his father and a resident of Lower Springs.

Lower Springs was two miles east of Shasta and rivaled Reading's Upper Springs in size. Lower Springs had its gold pockets and mining area. In 1853, Benjamin Swasey filed a land claim for 160 acres there. The house pictured was on this property, beautified with peach trees, vineyards, and palms.

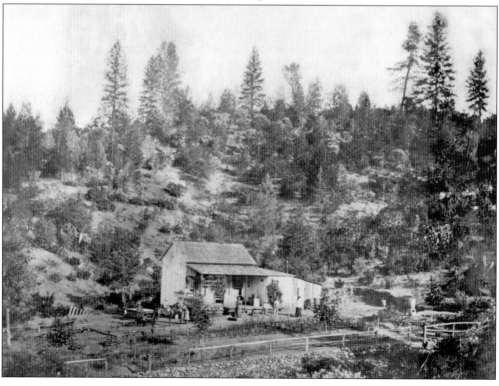

In 1861, Henry Blum married Mary A. Garrecht in the bride's
Shasta home, with Justice of the Peace C. C. Bush officiating.
The bride and groom were German. Henry had become
a naturalized American citizen in 1859, but Mary had
only arrived with her family in 1860. Henry Blumb
built his Blumb Bakery of frame construction and
opened it in 1878. The bakery served Shastans for
more than 50 years.

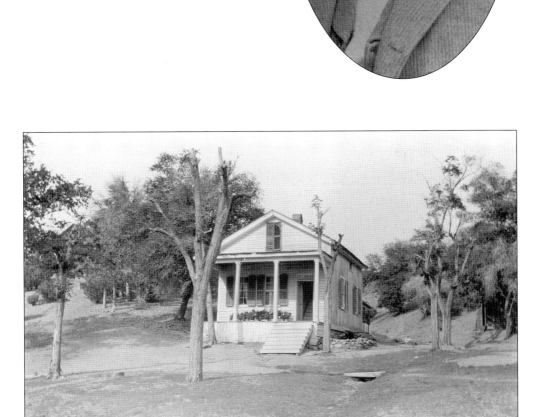

This tiny board and batten house, built by Everett French Crocker, contains seven rooms,
five downstairs and two up. Henry and Mary Garrecht raised their family of three girls and
two boys here.

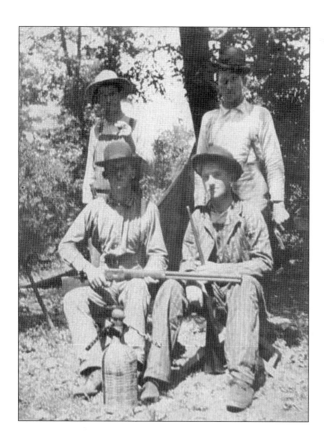

Young Shastans enjoy their weapons and wine, hopefully not together!

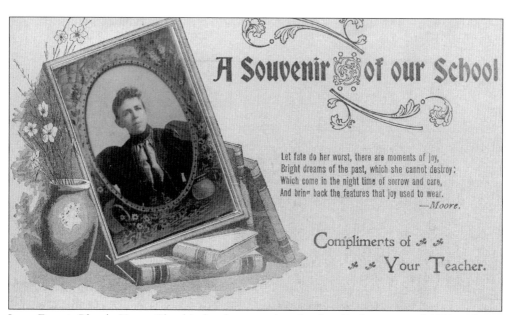

A Souvenir of our School

Let fate do her worst, there are moments of joy,
Bright dreams of the past, which she cannot destroy:
Which come in the night time of sorrow and care,
And bring back the features that joy used to wear.
— *Moore.*

Compliments of ✄ ✄

✄ ✄ Your Teacher.

Lena Francis Blumb, Henry Blumb's daughter, taught school at Buckeye around 1890 and sent her students home at the end of the term with this souvenir—a photograph of their teacher. At the age of 40, Lena Blumb married James Oliver.

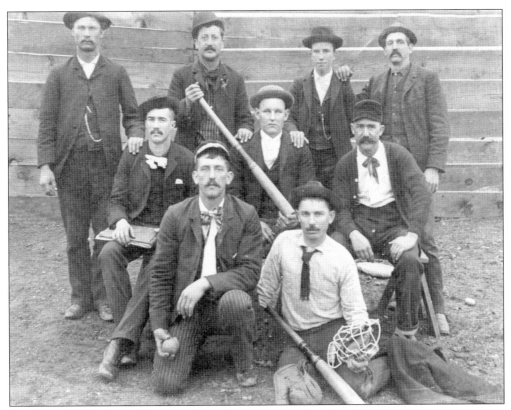

By the mid-1880s, baseball was reaching the status of America's favorite game. The exact origin of the sport is widely disputed, but organized teams began to appear around California in conjunction with the gold rush. The Shasta Red Stockings were one of many teams started by settlers from the East. Most teams consisted of 9 to 11 players that competed against squads from surrounding towns. Pictured, from left to right, are (first row) Grant Schroter (pitcher) and M. Foster (catcher); (second row) Chris Pharris (first base), Ed Isaacks (left field), and Charles Joseph Litsch (right field); (third row) Frank Tucker (short stop), W. Heffelfinger (second base), Ray McDonald (third base), and Kinder Schroter (left field).

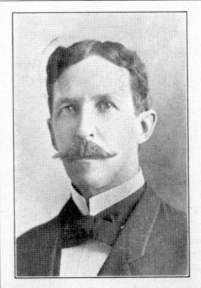

ROBERT L. READING

REGULAR DEMOCRATIC NOMINEE FOR

COUNTY SURVEYOR

SEARCHLIGHT, REDDING   ELECTION, NOV. 6

Robert L. Reading, son of Pierson Barton Reading, was a civil engineer, architect, and bridge designer. Redding's Free Bridge was his design and, in 1907, the longest steel span structure in California. He served as Shasta County surveyor from 1904 through 1916.

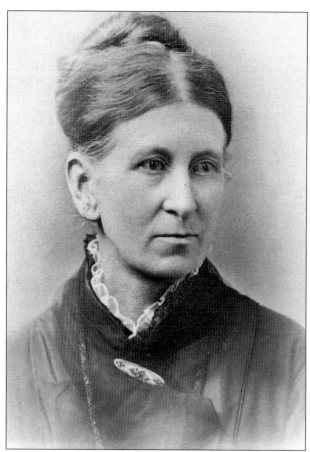

Normal school training in New York enabled Donna Evans to teach in the spring of 1857 in Shasta's first schoolhouse, built in December 1854. She continued to teach until the end of 1861, when she married Advram Coleman, the Shasta merchant who had taken over the business of the Bull, Baker, and Company. In 1875, Mrs. Coleman was appointed to the Office of County Superintendent of Schools of Shasta County. Prior to this appointment, only men had held the position. In fact, she was the first woman to hold that position in the entire state of California! Mrs. Coleman served five elected terms in the position—a total of 11 years—defeated for a sixth term by one of her former students, Eliza Welch. During her tenure as superintendent, Mrs. Coleman created changes and innovations that made Shasta County schools compare favorably with any in the state. After her defeat, she returned to the classroom until 1890.

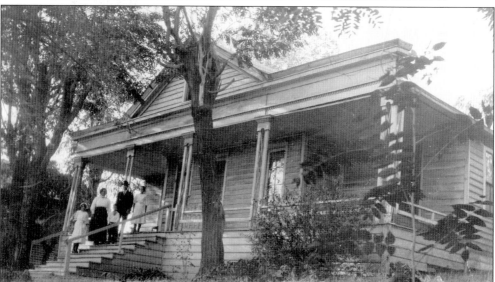

The home of Advram and Donna Coleman stood on a large lot between the Spragues and the Brunnings. Purchased shortly after their marriage, they were the sixth owners in only seven years "indicating the extreme fluidity of life in Shasta." Howard, their only son, was raised here.

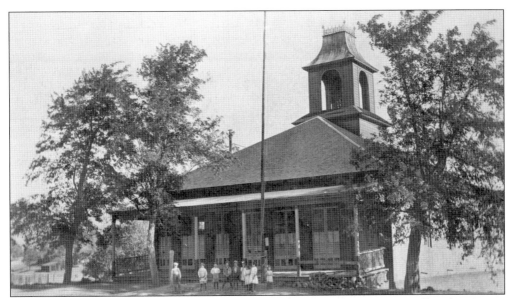

In 1875, Donna Coleman taught in this brick schoolhouse. Francis Carr, principal/teacher; Hettie Pryor; and Susie Cadwell taught also. Their students included the Litsches, the Leschinskys, the Johnsons, the Wellendorfs, the Hoppings, the Garrechts, the Blumbs, the Grotefends, and the Lewins—an ethnically diverse and integrated group.

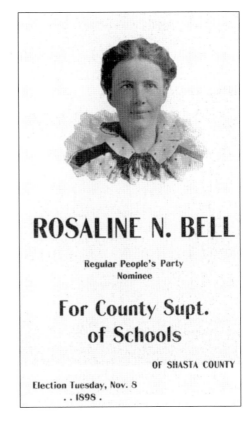

ROSALINE N. BELL

Regular People's Party Nominee

For County Supt. of Schools

OF SHASTA COUNTY

Election Tuesday, Nov. 8 . . 1898 .

Rosaline Bell was a part of Judge Aaron Bell's family. She taught in 1894 at the Eastside Grammar School in Redding.

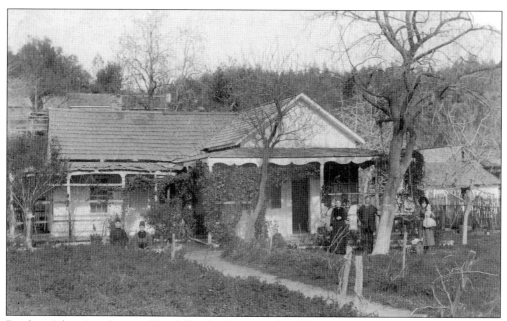

Brothers John, Augustus, and Jacob Leschinsky arrived in Shasta in 1849 as locksmith/blacksmith, merchant/gardener, and farmer respectively. They homesteaded, married, and had children in the area. This is a photograph of the home of Augustus Leschinsky with Eda, August, and Johanna standing underneath a tree.

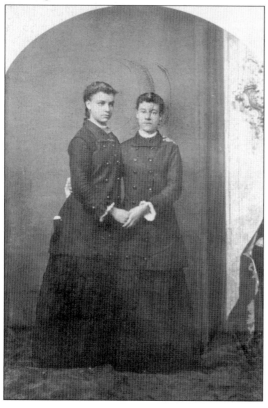

Sisters Mary and Tilly Leschinsky pose for a formal family portrait. Mary became the wife of James Edward Isaacs in 1882 and his widow in 1932.

In 1855, James Edward Isaacs was born in Shasta. His running mates, barefoot youngsters in a mining camp, were George and Charlie Shurtleff, Ed Sweeney, Frank Swasey, the Grotefend boys, and Ed Gage. He studied law under the celebrated Clay W. Taylor and upon his death, was described as "lawyer, journalist, wit, a leading politician of the Jeffersonian persuasion and a fraternal friend of mankind."

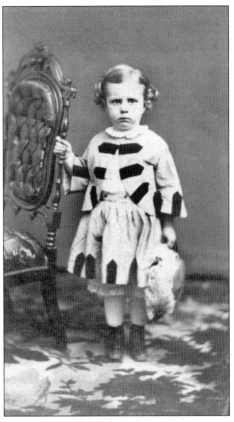

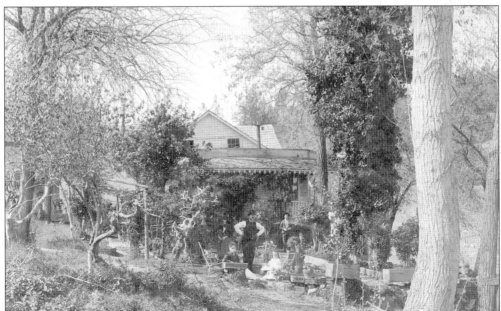

A. L. Downer built this home in Shasta. His daughter Celinda married Joseph Isaacs of Hollub and Isaacs. This 1888 photograph is of Celinda's son James Edward Isaacs, his wife, Mary Leschinsky Isaacs, and their daughter Linnie. Both James and his daughter Linnie were born in this house.

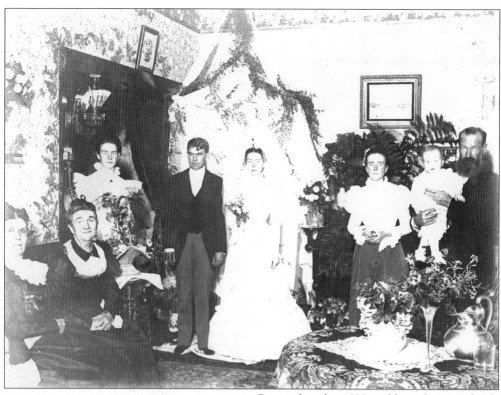

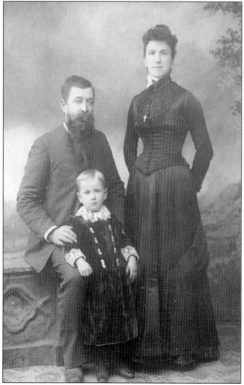

Pictured in this 1899 wedding photograph of Ruth Bell and Louis Garrecht, from left to right, are (seated) Amelia Garrecht and Mary Bell; (standing) Mary Bell, Louis Garrecht, Ruth Bell Garrecht, Jennie Bell, Uncle Joseph Bell, and baby Edmund Bell.

Pictured are Sylvester Hull, his second wife, Celina Zorn Hull, and their son Milton, who died young.

Martha Whiting, daughter of Capt. Danforth Whiting, married Sylvester Hull. Martha died in 1876 leaving two children, Sam and Eva (Evelina).

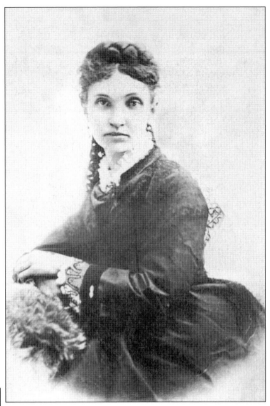

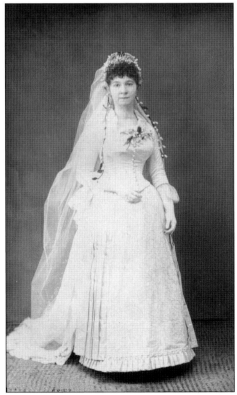

Eva Hull, daughter of Sylvester Hull and Martha Whiting Hull, was not only well-educated and an accomplished pianist, but also an acknowledged Shasta beauty. She is pictured as the bride of a Mr. Lauder.

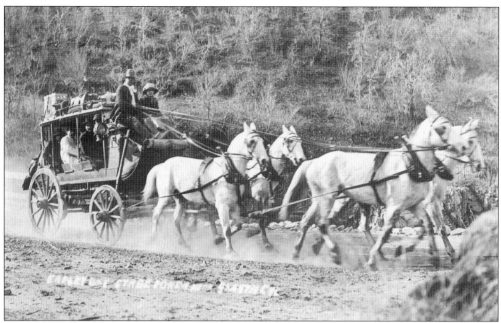

No class of western men was more entitled to knighthood than the stage driver. A stage driver had the responsibility not only for the lives of his passengers and the management of spirited horse teams over rugged terrain, but also the commerce and mail of merchants, bankers, and brokers.

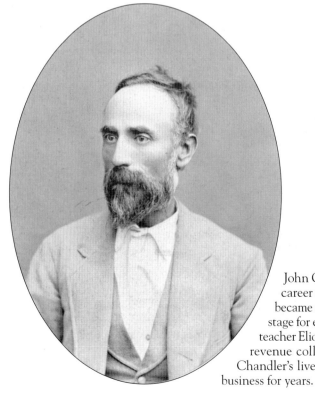

John Craddock began his "transportation" career as an Illinois stable boy, but at 21 he became a stage driver in 1853 Shasta. He drove stage for eight years. Craddock married Shasta teacher Eliot Chauncey, served as a United States revenue collector in 1862, and purchased F. B. Chandler's livery stable in Shasta, conducting this business for years.

John E. Reynolds, age 10, rode the "bell horse" of a pack train from Shasta to Douglas City. Each teamster belled his lead horses and from the tone, the driver knew who and where he was to be met on the narrow roads. At 16, Reynolds began driving stage and continued until he became a messenger for Wells Fargo Express Company. Reynolds was known as a man without fear and his career was marked by thrilling episodes. Twice Wells Fargo awarded his bravery. In 1884, Sheriff W. E. Hopping "in appreciation of his fearlessness and bravery under fire" appointed him undersheriff.

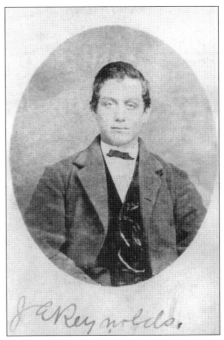

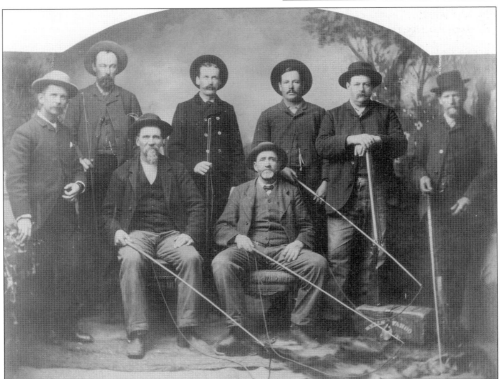

These men were "Knights of the Whip," or stage drivers. The stage driver's whip, gloves, and hat were emblematic of their profession and quite distinctive. Their fine buckskin gloves were handmade by women in Shasta catering specially to that trade. This photograph celebrates the stage drivers and their cargo, often the signature Wells Fargo and Company box.

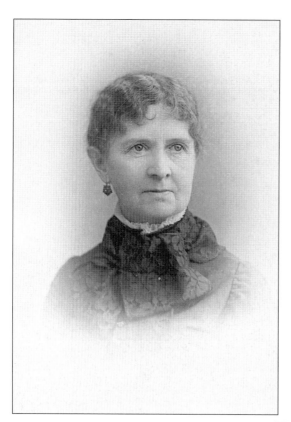

The widowed Sarah Elizabeth Smith Bacon visited her sons and brother W. L. Smith in Shasta and returned with the remainder of her family in 1870. Her sons worked for the California Stage Company and her brother was the division agent. Her daughters were Mildred Bacon Bartlett, the second Mrs. Louis Wellendorf, and Mae Helene Bacon Boggs, "patron saint of Shasta State Historic Park."

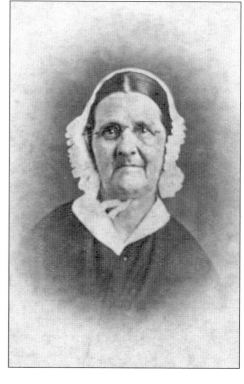

Susan Geiger was the mother of Vincent Geiger, who with others established the Pioneer Pie Factory in Shasta. Their sole business was the manufacture and sale of peach pies described as having upper and lower crusts "a little too near together." No doubt the peaches were from the orchards of Ben Swasey.

W. L. Carter began his publishing career at 17 in Illinois with a newspaper he called the *Prairie Pioneer*. On the Pacific Coast, another newspaper, the *Shasta Courier* was printing stories he chose, too. In 1860, Carter came overland to mine unsuccessfully in Shasta. In 1864, he established the newspaper, the *Copper City Pioneer*. In 1869, he purchased the *Shasta Courier*, becoming its third editor. After much merging and consolidation, the paper moved to Redding and ultimately became the *Record Searchlight*.

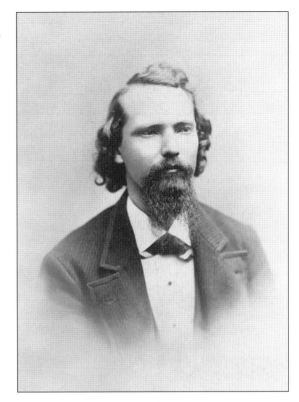

In 1861, Ella Gage, eldest daughter of Jonathan and Alice Gage, taught at the Shasta school for African American children. In 1867, she married W. L. Carter.

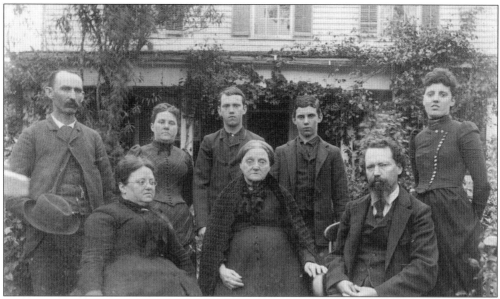

This is the W. L. Carter family—all Shasta pioneers grown old. Seated, from left to right, are (first row) Mrs. W. L. Carter (Ella Gage), Mrs. Jonathan Gage (Nelly or Alice Jane Swasey Gage), and W. L. Carter (newspaper owner); (second row) Joe Carter (W. L.'s brother), Mrs. C. H. Darling (W. L.'s daughter), Lloyd L. Carter, Milton G. Carter (W. L.'s sons), and Mrs. Briceland Blair (W. L.'s daughter).

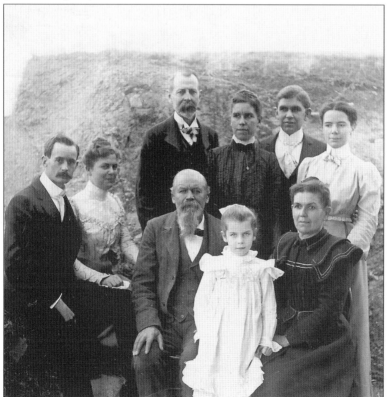

This is the extended Lorenz Garrecht family of Shasta. Pictured, from left to right, are (first row) Will Schoonover, Nell Schoonover, Lorenz Garrecht, Nelda Briggs, and Amelia Garrecht; (second row) Carl Briggs, Anna Briggs, Louie Garrecht, and Ruth Garrecht.

Lloyd L. Carter, W. L. Carter's eldest son, joined his father in the newspaper business, making the *Shasta Courier* a family affair.

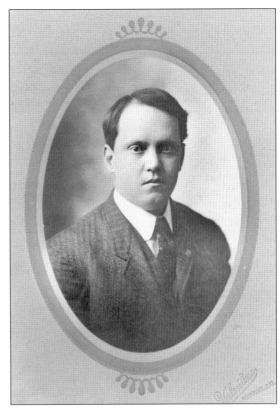

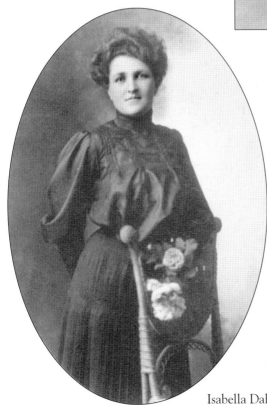

Isabella Dahlen Carter was Lloyd's wife.

Ethel Carter Blair much later married Briceland Blair and even later became an editor and partner in the family newspaper. She died in 1949.

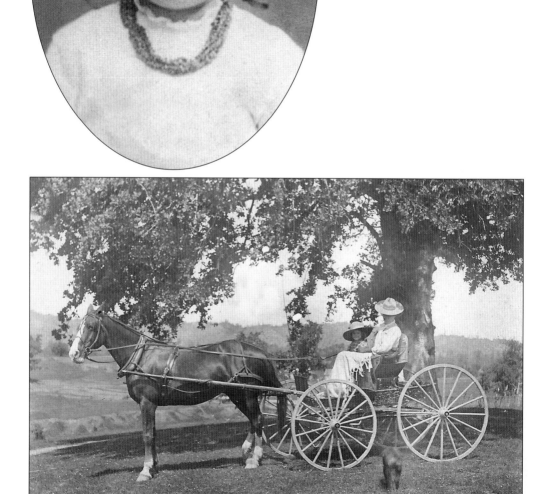

Ruth and her daughter Ruth Garrecht take a buggy ride near their home in Shasta.

In 1875, Ellen Meta Wills, daughter of W. S. Wills, married Arthur Hale Sprague. She died leaving three children.

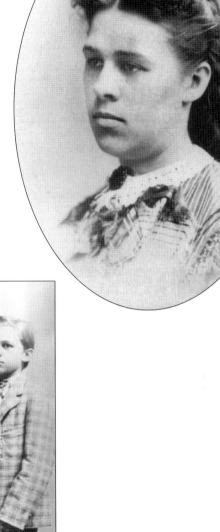

Arthur, Anna, and Roy Sprague were the children of Arthur and Ellen Sprague. She recalls her father was strict with them and set high standards. Anna was not allowed to read Charles Dickens as he "gave too crude a portrayal of life," but she did so anyway. Arthur, Anna, and Roy had good educations in Shasta and did well in the world.

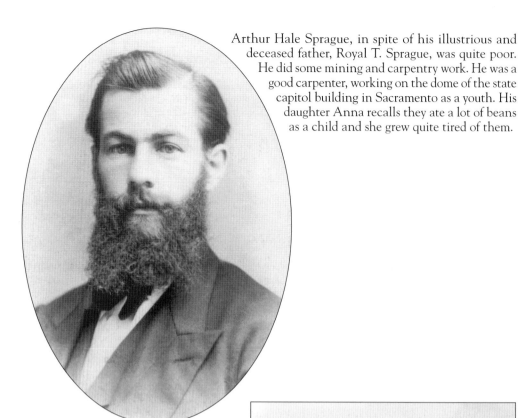

Arthur Hale Sprague, in spite of his illustrious and deceased father, Royal T. Sprague, was quite poor. He did some mining and carpentry work. He was a good carpenter, working on the dome of the state capitol building in Sacramento as a youth. His daughter Anna recalls they ate a lot of beans as a child and she grew quite tired of them.

Elizabeth Eames, wife of Shasta blacksmith Charles Eames and mother of several children, including Willie, pictured here, took over the Higinbotham Gallery when the owner was away mining, and made studio photographs.

Five

ONE TOUGH TOWN

Crimes in Shasta, big and small, pervaded much of the news of the 1850s. With personal fortunes coming and going so quickly, hard-luck miners often resorted to petty theft and when caught claimed they were only "borrowing the goods." Thievery was common and stories about the latest heists filled the newspaper. No one was safe, not even the sheriff, from small acts of theft. Sheriff Nunnally reported that while he slept, a "gentleman" entered his house and made off with "a very valuable gold watch, a gold pencil, a key to a pair of handcuffs and eighty dollars in money." Nunnally was so upset over the loss that he placed an ad in the newspaper offering a $100 for the return of the watch.

Gambling played a major role in the entertainment of gold miners in the hotels and saloons of Shasta. Along with this gambling always came the temptation to cheat, which if detected, usually meant violent retribution. One incident at the Trinity House, where several gambling tables indulged players day and night, ended in deadly violence and the subsequent trial that had the town buzzing for weeks. According to one account, James Nolan, the dealer at the table, wrongly drew several cards and cheated one of the players, Alex Murdock, of $40. The following account reveals what happened next:

> A dispute then ensued, Mr. M (Murdock) in the mildest manner, demanding to be treated fairly in the game. At this time Mr. M. had his hand upon his pistol as it hung in his scabbard by his side. N. (Nolan) however refused to return the money, but left his seat and went behind the bar, where, without its being noticed, he secured a pistol and walking up to Mr. M. said, "you have a pistol, defend yourself," accompanying the words, or rather preceding them; with a shot. Mr. M. dropped almost instantaneously dead. The ball entered the upper lobe of the right lung, passed through the aorta, or main artery, thence striking the back bone on the right side, passed between the third and fourth ribs, and rested in the muscles of the back.

Immediately after the fatal shot the murderer conducted himself in a manner brutal and unfeeling to a degree almost incredible—dancing, jumping and laughing around his victim with the greatest glee and boasting of the deed as one of his "jobs." His only excuse for the act was, that Mr. M. had his pistol in his hand at the time, and he did the act in self-defense.

At the subsequent trial Nolan's own partner, friends, and associates testified that Murdock did not make a movement to use his pistol. The jury acted quickly and ordered Nolan to be hanged. Before putting the rope around his neck, Nolan admitted that he did not think that Murdock was going to use his pistol. Nolan's execution is noted as follows:

> Owing to the knot having been placed improperly, when the trap door fell the rope drew against the side of his chin, and he consequently died a most horrible death, struggling an unusual length of time while hanging. Thus ended the life of a young but very bad-hearted man.

Law and order was, in the early days of the community, maintained by one or more sheriffs and whatever deputies he could sign on. Sheriffs were elected, sometimes by informal vote, and performed their duties until the next election or until they asked to step down. Robbery appears to be the crime most frequently mentioned in historical record, with murder cases or crimes involving American Indians or Chinese as the most talked about in town.

Uppermost in the minds of many Shastans during the 1850s was ongoing concern over American Indians. They saw American Indians as the single greatest threat to law and order and they organized armed posses to deal with the growing threat. According to local residents, wandering groups of Pitt River Indians were responsible for a series of robberies and murders on the Sacramento Trail. Mass meetings were held in which heated debate tried to answer the following question: "What course shall the Whites pursue toward the Indians of Northern California?" It was common for the citizens of Shasta to refer to local American Indians as savages and to think that "every day [they] are becoming more daring in their attacks upon the property as well as the lives of our people." By 1854–1855, the biggest problem appears to have been the perception that the American Indians were carrying on a hit-and-run tactic of warfare along the various roads leading to the town. Townspeople believed that the American Indians had escalated their acts of robbery to that of murder against any and all whites found traveling on isolated roads. According to one resident, American Indians were "no longer confining themselves to the perpetration of mere acts of theft, they are boldly and at every opportunity slaying our citizens."

Most Shasta citizens surmised that American Indians were desperate for food and clothing. One report noted that the Wintuns' supply of acorns had been exhausted, thus forcing them to search out other sources of food. The popular course of action to take with American Indians had always been force, notwithstanding treaties protecting native lives. Public debate on this issue usually climaxed with an agreement to form a vigilante force to seek out and kill American Indians. One townsperson said it succinctly, "The only sure way then of accomplishing this desirable result is by means of force. They must be whipped—if needs be, exterminated." Despite the ardent attempts of some area residents, such as Pierson B. Reading, the majority of Shasta citizens agreed with the policy of using force against American Indians. The resulting action by Shasta vigilantes usually resulted in some American Indians being killed and the rest being "chased into the hills."

Chinese living in the area were, at times, targets of violence particularly if it was known that they had recently struck gold or were in possession of money. Such was the case in December 1853, when bandits attacked a group of Chinese miners lodged just south of town. The surprised miners yelled for help, yet a group of nearby white miners could not understand what the Chinese were saying and they surmised that it must be a "drunken frolic." By the time help did arrive, they found the Chinese "horribly mutilated and tied to the wheel of a wagon." One of the men had been cut across the neck, but the bleeding was stopped and he survived. The other man "had his head and face cut in a most shocking manner." Afterward it was learned that the assailants had robbed the Chinese of $300 by cutting off a money belt that one of the Chinese had been wearing. For awhile, it was supposed that Joaquin Murrieta and his gang of thugs had done the terrible deed. However, the attackers turned out to be white drifters who ran south, but were captured and brought to trial in Red Bluff.

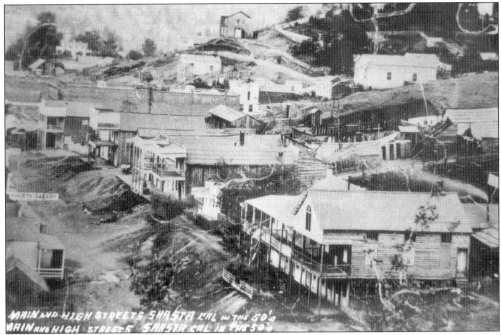

In September 1850, the men of Shasta County elected their first assemblyman, county judge, and justice of the peace. Although Reading's Rancho, located a few miles from Shasta, had served as the first county seat, by 1851, the seat of government moved to Shasta. In January 1854, the townspeople approved a contract to build Shasta's first courthouse, a two-story log building, for $5,280. It is pictured above in the top center of the photograph.

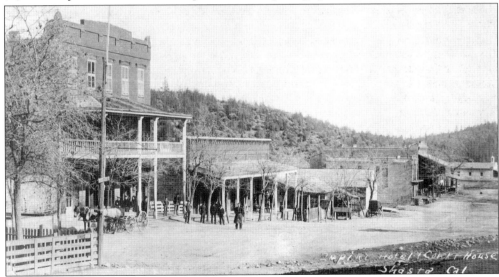

A demand was placed on the Shasta County government to provide more services. In 1861, county officials purchased a large brick building (pictured second from the left) to accommodate the needs of the prosperous, populous community. This building was purchased from James Loag for $25,000. After evicting three tenants and remodeling, county officials were open for business. This building served as the Shasta County Courthouse from 1862 to 1888, when the county seat was moved to Redding.

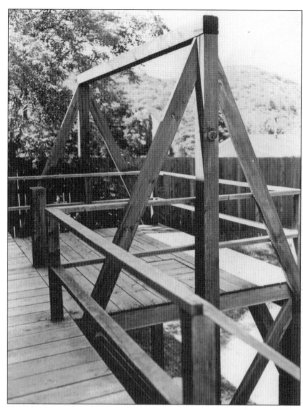

According to the *Shasta Courier* on August 29, 1874, "The scaffold, well built and in excellent working order, stood in the jail yard, completed, and covered over with canvas, to hide the same from public view . . . the prisoner's arms were strapped down...the iron door swings open and the condemned walk firmly upon the scaffold and take chairs on one side of the platform."

The inscription on the back of this photograph reads, "I don't know who this is, but think he was killed during a stage hold up in the early 80s west of Shasta."

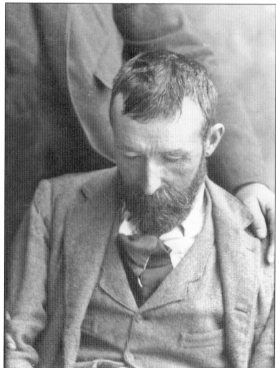

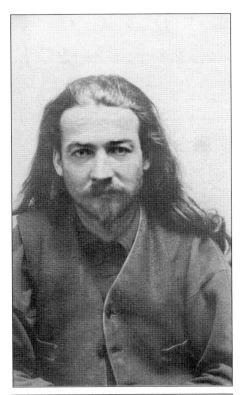

There was largely a "no tolerance" approach to crime in Shasta. Everyone worked hard and did not want to lose precious time dealing with thieves or murderers. Those who committed serious crimes were hanged, while less serious criminals received lashes. Miners who took it upon themselves to punish criminals sometimes branded, clipped ears, or dunked the offender in an icy stream. The Shasta jail was always kept busy. As many as 18 prisoners were housed at one time in the small jail. Written on the backs of the photographs on this page are the words, "in Shasta jail, 1888 for robbery."

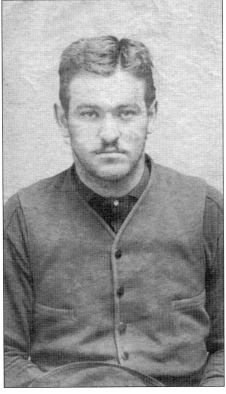

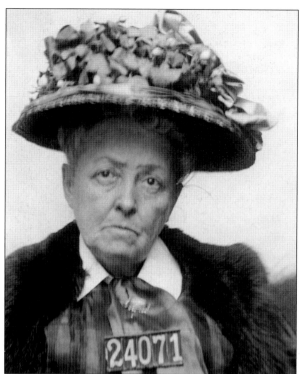

This photograph is from a prison logbook and only identifies this woman as prisoner number 24071. Another female prisoner, Mary Parker, arrested for drunk and disorderly conduct, served 20 days in jail in Shasta.

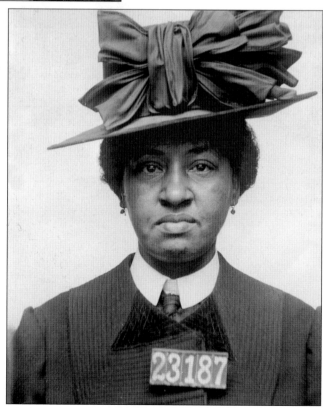

Another example of an unknown prisoner identified as prisoner number 23187 in an area jail log book.

$250 REWARD.

WANTED FOR ROBBERY AND MURDER.

F. S. EDDINGER alias GILMORE for murder of Ed Jose, at Lewiston, Trinity Co., California, on night of June 10th, 1894. Description—Height, 5 feet, 10 inches; weight, 175 pounds; light eyes; slightly stooped shouldered; wore thick sandy beard, (may shave); inveterate pipe smoker; teamster; generally carried money in shot sack; has wife and family at Angels Camp, Calaveras Co., Cal.

Arrest and telegraph:

A. F. ROSS, Sheriff of Shasta Co., Cal. or
JAS. BOWIE, Sheriff of Trinity Co., Cal.

Shasta served as the county seat for 27 years, and the museum archives reflect evidence of that fact. Arrest and wanted posters were routinely sent to the Shasta County sheriff, as well as throughout California. Although the county seat moved to Redding in 1888, the jail continued to be used in Shasta. Reward posters continued to be circulated as late as 1894.

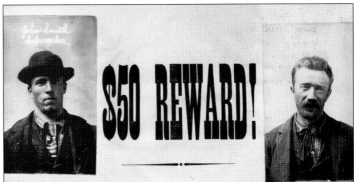

$50 REWARD!

TOM WILSON, with several aliases, a professional burglar and safe craker and John Smith his "pal," broke jail on the night of April 23d, for the second time. Description—Tom Wilson; age about 35 years; height about 5 feet 7 inches; well built; weight about 165 lbs; red or sandy coase hair, inclined to stand up; large blue eyes; straight nose; large mouth; sandy complexion; short stiff sandy beard. Dress—Snuff colored coat; blue overalls; checkered shirt; small black felt hat; had on right ankle an "Oregon boot."

JOHN SMITH; age about 22 years; height about 5 feet 6 or 7 inches; weight about 180 lbs; light hair, cut short; dark gray or hazel eyes; straight nose; small mouth, with mole below right corner; face rather pale, but has a set, determined expression; no beard. Had on dark coat; blue overalls; a small black felt hat, and an "Oregon boot" on right ankle.

Will give $25 for the arrest and detention of either, or $50 for the two escapes. These men were committed for carrying burglars tools, and are dangerous men. Arrest and notify

S. E. INLOW, Sheriff

Marysville, April 25th, 1893.   Yuba Co., Cal.

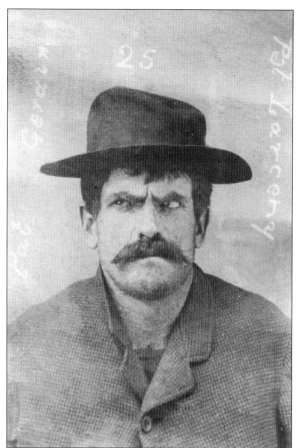

Not all of the justice conducted in Shasta was legal. Although this prisoner is unknown, he was fortunate to have been processed through the judicial system. In 1865, another prisoner, Pete Little, stabbed a man named Moran to death in a saloon brawl. In the confusion, Little escaped. However, the miners caught up with him and forced Little into a burlap sack filled with rocks and threw him into the river.

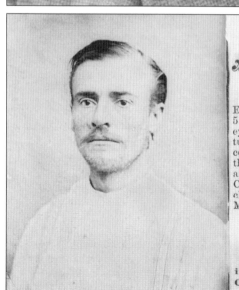

August 18th, 1883.

ARREST FOR MURDER

JAMES R. DOLLAR,

Ex convict, native of North Carolina; age 32; height 5 feet, 10 inches; weight 133 pounds; hair dark brown; eyes dark brown; dark florid complexion, square features, wide jaws, small scar on upper lip, light brown colored moustache when last seen, scar base of left thumb, large scar near left elbow, mole back left upper arm, slim built; served 9 years for Robbery from Napa County; sentenced to San Quentin July 3d, 1877; discharged June 3d, 1883. Last seen in San Francisco, Monday, August 13th. Arrest and telegraph at once to

P. CROWLEY,

Chief of Police, San Francisco.

The Photograph of Dollar attached was taken in 1877. DON'T POST THIS IN PUBLIC. For Officers only.

In 1883, Sheriff W. E. Hopping received this wanted poster with the instructions not to post it in public, but to arrest the wanted man and telegraph the chief of police in San Francisco at once to let him know that suspect had been apprehended.

Clay Webster Taylor was elected Shasta County district attorney from 1870 to 1882. He was described as a forceful trial lawyer, a fine orator, and possessed a magnetic personality, giving him great influence with juries and judges.

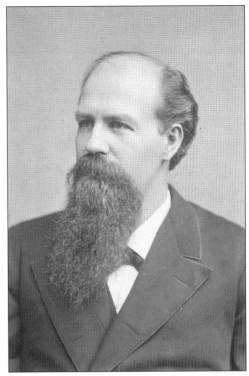

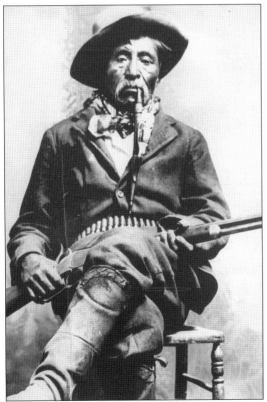

During the 1870s, "Indian Charley" Pit was a popular guide, tracker, and doctor in the Shasta area. After a Wells Fargo stage from Shasta was robbed in July 1877, he and Sisson Jim, another American Indian doctor, tracked down and captured the outlaws. Indian Charley is pictured here with a rifle that was given to him by Wells Fargo as a reward. The inscription on the rifle reads, "W. F. & Co. to Indian Charley for Capturing Highway Robber July 21, 1877." The rifle is a Model 1873 Winchester. It is a special-order rifle with a longer than standard barrel and a set trigger. Sisson Jim was also given a rifle that was buried with him.

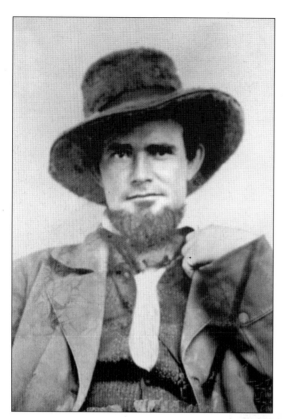

Henry Clay Stockton (1826–1884) was county sheriff from 1857 to 1859. Although his tenure was short, Stockton's strong leadership played an important role in the Chinese/white miner conflict of 1859. In a bold and calculated move, Stockton appealed to the governor for assistance. The arrival of 113 guns, additional ammunition, and the promise of troops quelled the fire of hostility. Stockton remained one of the few county officials to defend the Chinese when anti-foreign sentiments ran high. Stockton eventually moved to Tehema County and then to Lassen County, where he died in 1884.

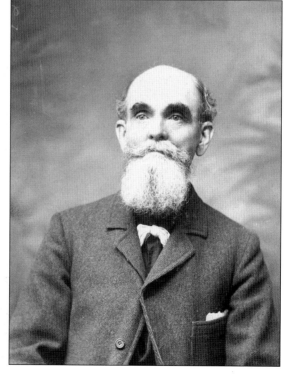

From 1867 to 1871, Thomas Greene served as Shasta County sheriff and tax collector. He was appointed county sheriff again in 1892 to complete William Hopping's term. He mined in the French Gulch area, owned the Empire Hotel, and, in 1881, operated Greene's Hotel.

Sylvester Hull (1831–1899) was Shasta County's sheriff and tax collector from 1871 to 1881. On the night of December 12, 1876, he and his deputies discovered five prisoners in the act of digging a hole to escape through the prison wall.

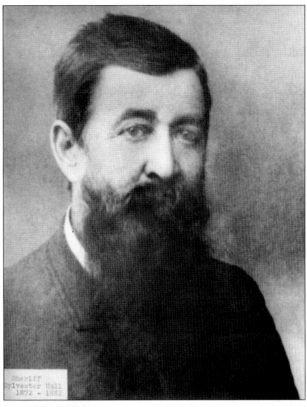

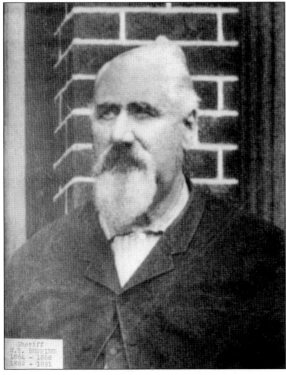

William Ely Hopping arrived early in 1852 to mine in the French Gulch area. He was twice elected as sheriff of Shasta County, from 1862 to 1866, and again from 1888 to 1892.

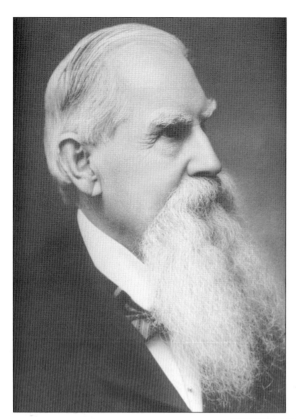

County judges rendered justice on a day-to-day basis, while the district judges were away. They heard lesser crimes and civil cases, probated uncontested wills, and issued temporary orders until the district judges returned. One notable judge was Chauncey Carroll Bush, who became a county judge in 1862 and served three terms until 1872. He then moved to Redding, where he is credited with building the first house and business. In addition to being involved in many civic affairs, C. C. Bush was unanimously elected Redding's first mayor.

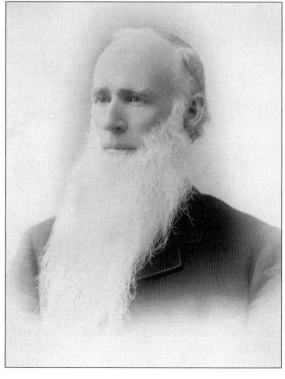

In 1880, California's new constitution combined county and district judge duties into one position—that of superior court justice. The constitution also allowed for at least one judge per county. Aaron Bell became the first superior court justice for Shasta County. He presided over one of the most hotly contested cases, the fate of the county seat. A highly charged election resulted in the decision to move the county seat to Redding. The citizens of Shasta refused to accept this and appealed to Judge Aaron Bell. He steadfastly upheld the election decision. The issue eventually went all the way to the Supreme Court, where Bell's ruling was upheld. In 1888, the county seat moved to Redding.

Six

SHASTA'S LEGACY

California gold-mining boomtowns of the 19th century rose quickly and usually faded just as quickly. San Francisco and Sacramento were two towns that in 1860 appeared to have avoided that trend and the citizens of Shasta hoped that their town would continue to flourish. However, ominous signs appeared by 1862. Placer mining played out in much of the county and in nearby Trinity County. By 1867, a corresponding decline in population left the town of Shasta with about 800 people. Many of the hard-luck miners realized that the real "gold" was in farming and scores of men purchased "good bottomland" in the Sacramento and San Joaquin Valleys. Other miners, bent on still striking it rich with gold, left for new gold fields that were being discovered in remote areas of the Sierra Nevada Mountains or Siskiyou County. Some left for Colorado and even to big new gold strikes in Alaska.

With gold drying up, Shasta business owners worried about their economic future. If their main business was catering to the gold miners and supplying goods and services to nearby gold-mining camps, what would happen now? The answer was simple enough. The saving event would be the coming of the railroad. With the conclusion of the Civil War, railroad construction was in full swing. A transcontinental railroad was completed in 1869 and Southern Pacific Railroad began building lines north and south from Sacramento. The plan called for unifying the state with a major trunk line running from San Diego in the south to Sacramento, and then on through Northern California to Portland, Oregon. Shasta's best chance for economic survival depended on the railroad coming through their town.

The summer of 1872 was the critical time period for determining Shasta's future. Railroad engineers from Southern Pacific surveyed the entire Sacramento River Valley and gorge to determine the most economically feasible route. Sadly for Shasta, railroad officials decided to undertake only a portion of the interstate connection for the time being and ended the northern terminus at the topographic head of the Sacramento Valley. Town leaders still hoped that this meant their town, but instead the railroad engineers chose a level location just five miles to the east—where the Sacramento River turns west. The terminal would sit on a bluff, high above the river, in an area previously known as Poverty Flats. Along with the railroad depot, Southern Pacific officials decided to build a new town, which they named the new hamlet Redding, in honor of Benjamin Bernard Redding, general land agent for Southern Pacific Railroad.

Shasta residents were devastated. Meetings were held to discuss what to do. Some business leaders such as Chauncy Carroll Bush saw the handwriting on the wall and decided to invest in the new business and home lots being sold by the Southern Pacific Railroad. Within a short time, he opened the first mercantile store in Redding. Following Bush's relocation, a slow exodus began. Hard times now hit the town with another devastating fire in 1878 that destroyed many of the remaining wooden structures. Residents, low on cash due to poor economic conditions, weighed the benefits of rebuilding. On top of this, gold revenues almost dried up completely by 1880. As Shasta shrank, Redding grew in size and population.

Despite the huge demographic shift, Shasta still retained the designation as county seat and thus remained a viable, important community. Yet this would change as well, once Redding civic leaders decided that the time had come to shift county government to their town. In 1882,

Redding proponents of the county seat change were able to get the issue on the ballot. A furious fight of words now began. Shasta leaders responded by claiming, "Redding is located in a low poisonous basin—a place where malaria abounds, and as a consequence the water cannot be drank." They went on to claim that the air in Redding was "suffocating during the hot summers months, and outside of the business stir of the place there is nothing pleasant or inviting in the entire section." The argument in favor of Shasta stretched to its limits when Shasta residents claimed their environment was "a healthy mountain Eden." Redding struck back, describing Shasta as a "has been" town, unable to sense its own decline. They also pointed out that the courthouse building was a "disaster waiting to happen."

The debate continued and the sides became clear. Shasta looked to the past, while Redding represented the railroad and the future. At the last minute, the tiny farming town of Millville was put on the ballot with Shasta and Redding for county seat, and just enough votes were siphoned off from Redding to win the election for Shasta. But Redding civic leaders only tried harder. Now they sought outside money and influence, and they waited for the 1886 election. By 1886, the population shift was lopsided and Redding easily won the bid to receive the county seat of government. With the removal of county government jobs from the town, Shasta's fate was sealed.

The 20th century dawned dimly for Shasta City, with only brief hopes for revival. A large gold find in 1901, at the "Old Diggings" site, spawned searches at all the old sites in and around the town. About that time, talk sizzled that a Redding to Eureka railroad was to be built and that there was a good chance that it would go through Shasta, but it never materialized. The copper boom of the World War I era bypassed the town as well. By 1920, a good number of vacant buildings began to crumble.

During the 1920s, concerned citizens in Shasta County began an effort to save the decaying buildings. Leadership for saving the community came from the Shasta Historical Society and Native Sons of the Golden West. One individual stands out during this time for dedicating time and money for the town's restoration—Mae Helene Bacon Boggs. Many of the dilapidated buildings were still held in private hands so she purchased land and structures for safe keeping. The California State Park Commission entered the scene in the 1930s and became interested in making Shasta into a state historic park.

Opened in 1950, the Courthouse Museum became the centerpiece of the new Shasta State Historic Park. The museum, restored to its 19th-century appearance contains artifacts that help visitors grasp what life was like during the gold rush and subsequent periods in the life of the town. A highlight of the museum today is the art collection donated by Mae Helene Bacon Boggs. This collection represents a wide variety of painting styles and includes a broad, ethnic look at life in Shasta from its earliest years.

Today preservation of the town of Old Shasta continues under the guidance of the California Department of Parks and Recreation, supported, in part, through efforts of the Town of Shasta Interpretive Association. A full range of educational activities are provided for tourists and local schools, including guided tours of the museum and the nearby cemeteries, baking demonstrations, and outdoor performances.

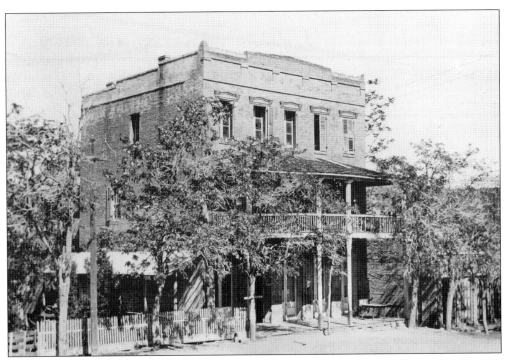

The Empire Hotel, built in 1857 at a cost of $30,000, was the largest hotel in Shasta. It was also in operation the longest. The scene of many social events, the Empire Hotel, was the center of important gatherings in the county. The building was torn down in 1920 and the bricks used as building material in Redding.

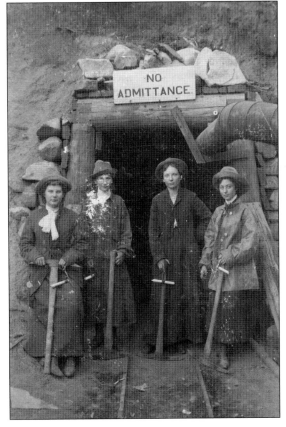

This photograph, taken at the entrance to the Brown Bear Mine in 1907, provides evidence that mining was still viable in Shasta County.

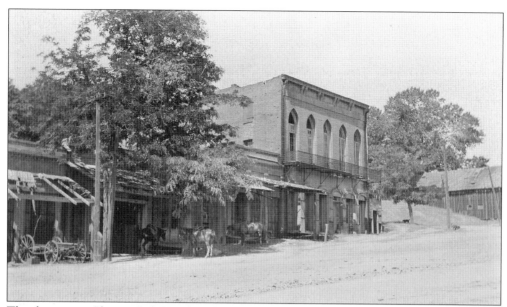

The three-story Charter Oak Hotel, with gothic windows and graceful wrought iron balconies, was surely the most beautiful building in Shasta. The ground floor contained a two-story grand ballroom. The back halves of the second and third floors were apartments. In 1915, the Charter Oak was dismantled and the unique yellow bricks hauled into Redding to build a new steam laundry.

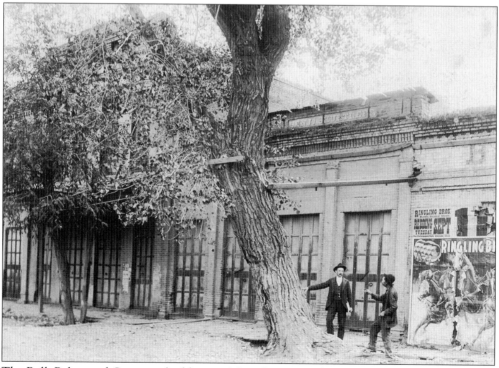

The Bull, Baker, and Company building on Main Street stood near the St. Charles Hotel, with 35 feet of frontage and a tin roof covered with 15 inches of dirt for further fire proofing.

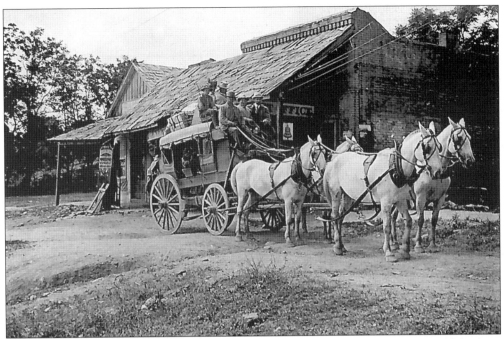

The Litsch Store acquired a reputation as a sort of museum with a collection of old fixtures, merchandise, records, and outdated stock.

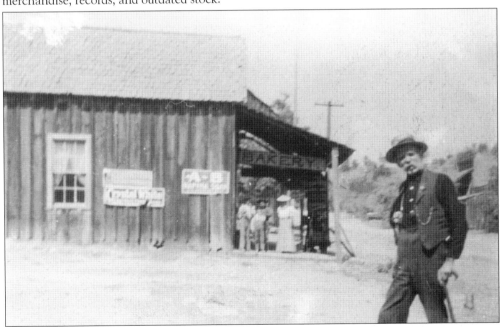

Pictured here is Henry Blumb shortly before his stroke. From 1873 to 1918, Blumb owned and operated his bakery, where it was customary for respectable elderly women to stop for a glass of beer after Sunday church. Blumb utilized a huge brick oven, heated with manzanita wood, which had the capacity to bake 150 loaves of bread at a time. In 1898, the loaves sold for three cents apiece. Henry Blumb, a very methodical man, made his daily trips from home to the bakery and back, never stepping out of the beaten path. He was in Redding only half a dozen times in his life.

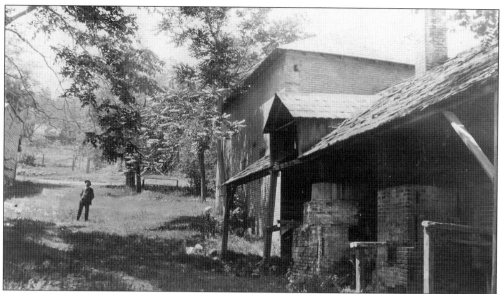

Although in ruins, the Washington Brewery, built in 1855, still stands at Shasta State Historic Park today.

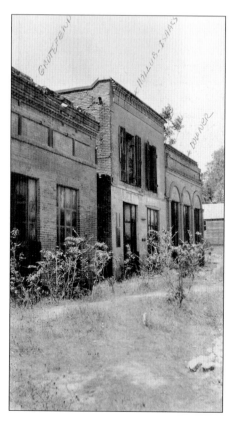

By the 1920s, long-abandoned buildings along Main Street fell into ruin. Many referred to Shasta as a ghost town.

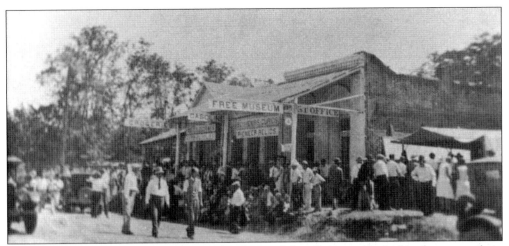

Shasta is shown in this parade photograph taken on Main Street, with the Litsch mercantile in the background. By 1922, the Litsch Store, the only general store left in operation, had become a museum as the signage reflects.

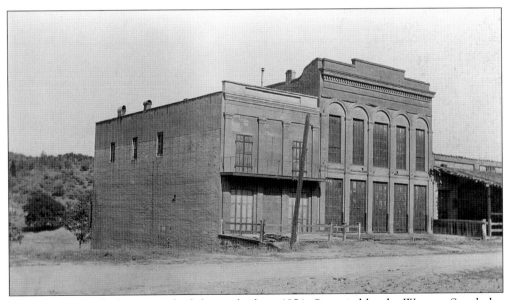

The Masonic Hall, shown on the left, was built in 1854. Occupied by the Western Star lodge No. 2 that same year, it contains the first Masonic charter brought to California in 1848 by Peter Lassen. This lodge is still active, offering a variety of fund-raisers and educational activities. The Armory Hall on the right housed various local businesses.

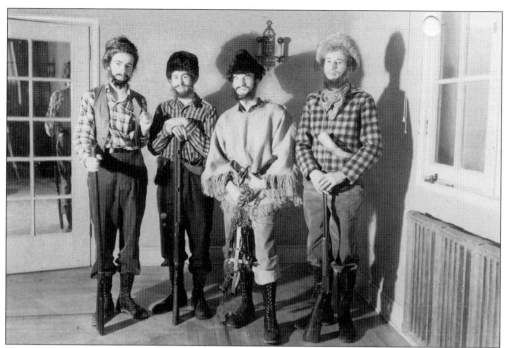

Trappers Alexander McLeod, Peter Ogden, P. B. Reading, and Jedediah Smith are portrayed by Shasta Historical Society members at their annual birthday party in 1937, held at the Golden Eagle Hotel in Redding.

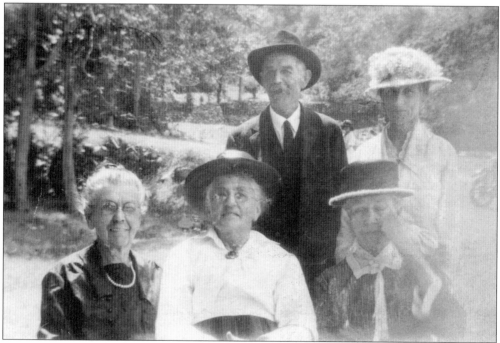

These pioneer families and their offspring, who came to Shasta and stayed, from left to right, are (first row) Amelia Garrecht, Eunice Blair, and Nellie Dobrowsky; (second row) Louis Prehn and Celina Hull.

Ethel Carter Blair grew up in Shasta, living in the Shurtleff mansion and playing with Anna Sprague. Later Blair partnered with her brother as editor of the *Shasta Courier*, which ultimately became the *Record Searchlight*.

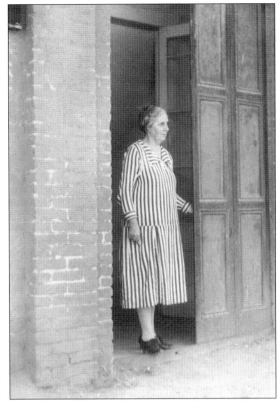

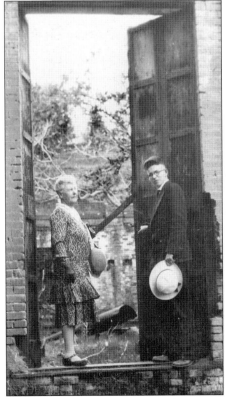

On the back of this photograph, the caption handwritten by Edna Behrens Eaton reads, "Saturday, April 20, 1930, Richard B. Eaton opening a door of the past to the future of Shasta 'Queen City of the North' for Mae Helene Bacon Boggs."

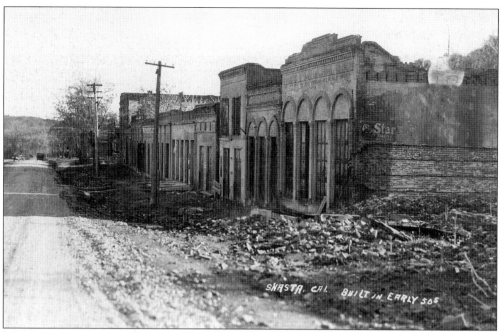

This is a view of the business district taken for a postcard in the 1950s. The ruins seen here remain today as Shasta's legacy.

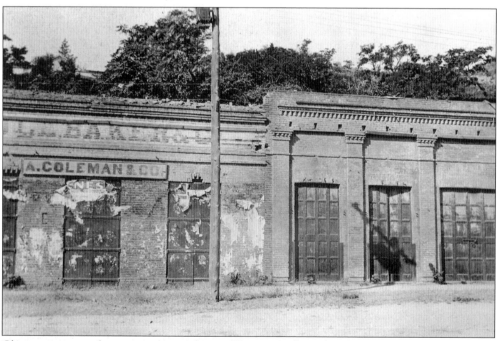

Changes in ownership were commonplace in Shasta as reflected in the signage—Bull, Baker, and Company became A. Coleman and Company in 1858 and was still operating in 1881.

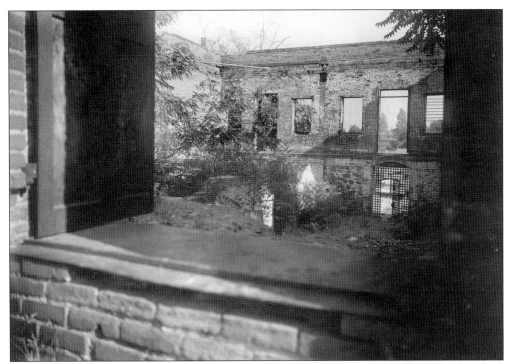

"The old courthouse a brick building in a fair state of preservation was built in 1855. The Native Sons will keep the old building in repair. They will try to restore it to keep its natural state and preserve it for all time. While many other brick buildings in the old town have been torn down to get building material, the old courthouse will stand forever," reported *The Searchlight* in March 1922.

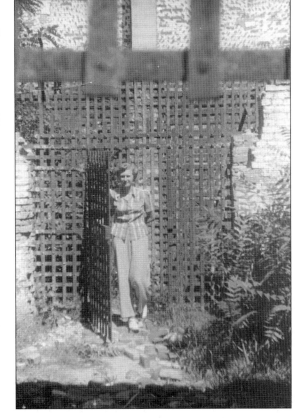

Visiting tourists found Shasta both a historic destination and a ghost town. This 1941 photograph of June Braucht was taken by her husband, Jess, during their honeymoon trip. They described the courthouse as being "a brick shell with no roof."

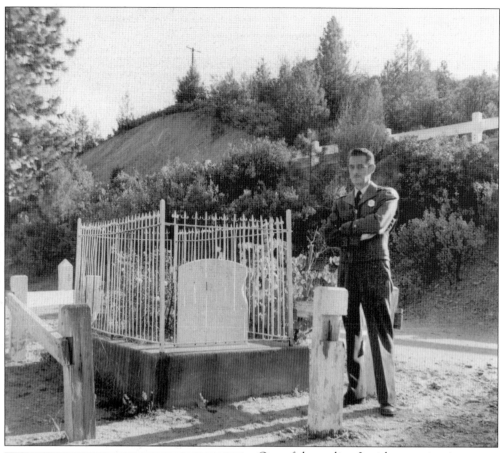

One of the earliest Jewish gravesites in Northern California dates to 1864. It is the final resting place of Charles Brownstein, second son of George and Helen Cohn Brownstein, who had emigrated from Poland. With no Jewish cemetery in Red Bluff, the Brownstein's had to journey a day over rough roads to bury their child in the Hebrew Association Cemetery, whose trustee was local Shasta merchant Emanuel Lewin.

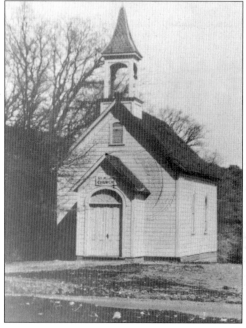

St. Mary's Chapel, built with money collected by Miss Louise Litsch, stood from 1903 to 1946 across from Father Rainaldi's stone foundation. The frame church, erected originally in 1852, was moved in 1854 to the foot of Cemetery Hill. Catholic Fathers Florian, Rainaldi, and O'Brien served their congregations from that frame church.

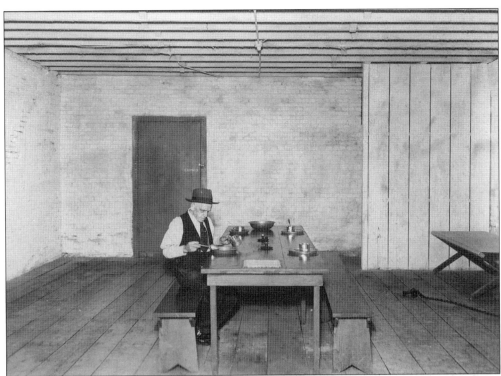

George Albro (1862–1955) started hanging around the courthouse in the 1870s and was hired as custodian soon thereafter. Albro played a role in early court proceedings. Crouch and Baker were hanged on gallows that Albro built. In 1884, George Albro was promoted to jailer. His career with Shasta County spanned 75 years, serving in many capacities. Albro kept items discarded by his employers. This pack rat trail, along with a keen memory, allowed accurate, historical placement of original furnishings during the courthouse renovation. Above, George Albro "dines" as prisoners did. Below, Albro stands with his collection of keys and locks.

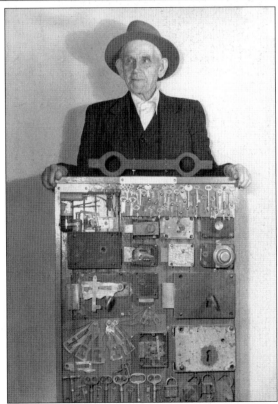

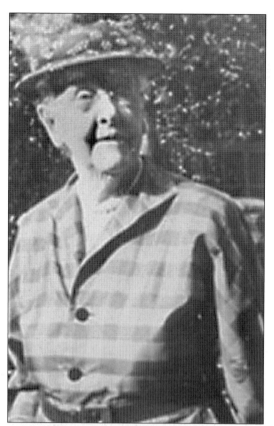

Mrs. Boggs was interested in making improvements for Redding, as well as Shasta. She is pictured here in front of the Redding Woman's Improvement Club, an organization dedicated to beautifying Redding. Mrs. Boggs gave the property for the site upon which their clubhouse was built. The club raised funds for new plants, flowers, trees, and road improvements.

Pictured in June 1950, from left to right, are Mrs. Boggs, unidentified, May Southern, unidentified, and Newton B. Drury. As part of the California and Shasta County Centennial Celebration, the town of Shasta and the courthouse were dedicated as Shasta State Historical Monument.

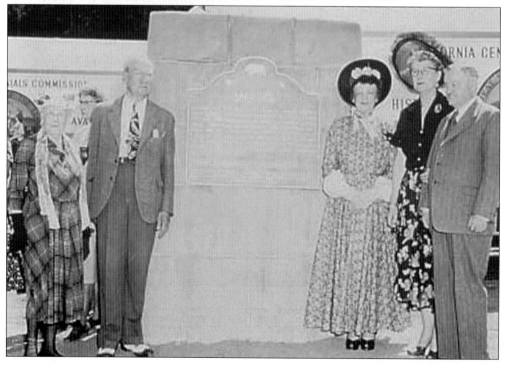

In 1922, after years of neglect, Shasta County supervisors sold the old courthouse building to the McCloud Parlor of the Native Sons of the Golden West for one dollar.

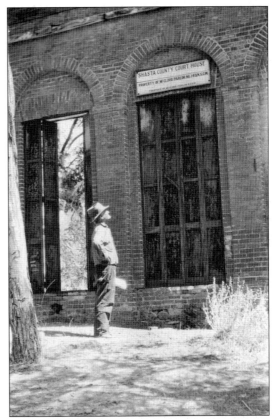

In 1950, the newly remodeled Courthouse Museum opened to the public under the direction of the California Division of Beaches and Parks.

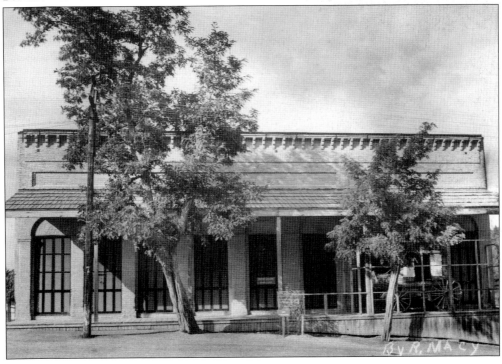

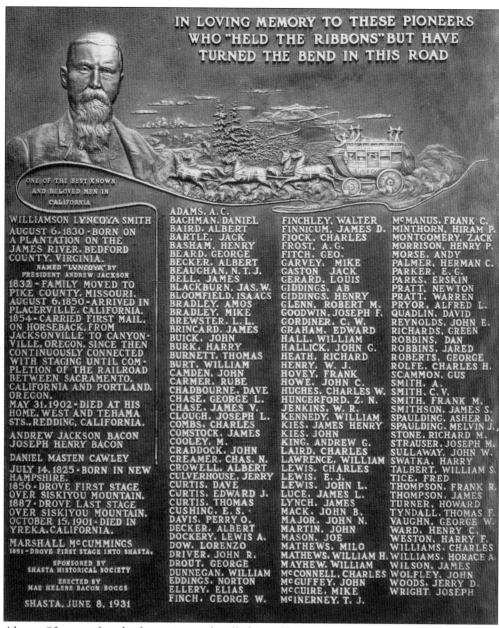

IN LOVING MEMORY TO THESE PIONEERS WHO "HELD THE RIBBONS" BUT HAVE TURNED THE BEND IN THIS ROAD

ONE OF THE BEST KNOWN AND BELOVED MEN IN CALIFORNIA

WILLIAMSON LYNCOYA SMITH
AUGUST 6, 1830 - BORN ON A PLANTATION ON THE JAMES RIVER, BEDFORD COUNTY, VIRGINIA.
NAMED "LYNCOYA" BY PRESIDENT ANDREW JACKSON
1832 - FAMILY MOVED TO PIKE COUNTY, MISSOURI.
AUGUST 6, 1850 - ARRIVED IN PLACERVILLE, CALIFORNIA.
1854 - CARRIED FIRST MAIL ON HORSEBACK, FROM JACKSONVILLE TO CANYON-VILLE, OREGON. SINCE THEN CONTINUOUSLY CONNECTED WITH STAGING UNTIL COM-PLETION OF THE RAILROAD BETWEEN SACRAMENTO, CALIFORNIA AND PORTLAND, OREGON.
MAY 31, 1902 - DIED AT HIS HOME, WEST AND TEHAMA STS., REDDING, CALIFORNIA.

ANDREW JACKSON BACON
JOSEPH HENRY BACON

DANIEL MASTEN CAWLEY
JULY 14, 1825 - BORN IN NEW HAMPSHIRE.
1856 - DROVE FIRST STAGE OVER SISKIYOU MOUNTAIN.
1887 - DROVE LAST STAGE OVER SISKIYOU MOUNTAIN.
OCTOBER 15, 1901 - DIED IN YREKA, CALIFORNIA.

MARSHALL McCUMMINGS
1851 - DROVE FIRST STAGE INTO SHASTA.

SPONSORED BY SHASTA HISTORICAL SOCIETY
ERECTED BY MAE HELENE BACON BOGGS

SHASTA, JUNE 8, 1931

ADAMS, A. C.
BACHMAN, DANIEL
BAIRD, ALBERT
BARTLE, JACK
BASHAM, HENRY
BEARD, GEORGE
BECKER, ALBERT
BEAUGHAN, N. T. J.
BELL, JAMES
BLACKBURN, JAS. W.
BLOOMFIELD, ISAACS
BRADLEY, AMOS
BRADLEY, MIKE
BREWSTER, L. L.
BRINCARD, JAMES
BUICK, JOHN
BURK, HARRY
BURNETT, THOMAS
BURT, WILLIAM
CAMDEN, JOHN
CARMER, RUBE
CHADBOURNE, DAVE
CHASE, GEORGE L.
CHASE, JAMES V.
CLOUGH, JOSEPH L.
COMBS, CHARLES
COMSTOCK, JAMES
COOLEY, M.
CRADDOCK, JOHN
CREAMER, CHAS. N.
CROWELL, ALBERT
CULVERHOUSE, JERRY
CURTIS, DAVE
CURTIS, EDWARD J.
CURTIS, THOMAS
CUSHING, E. S.
DAVIS, PERRY O.
DECKER, ALBERT
DOCKERY, LEWIS A.
DOW, LORENZO
DRIVER, JOHN R.
DROUT, GEORGE
DUNNEGAN, WILLIAM
EDDINGS, NORTON
ELLERY, ELIAS
FINCH, GEORGE W.

FINCHLEY, WALTER
FINNICUM, JAMES D.
FIOCK, CHARLES
FROST, A. G.
FITCH, GEO.
GARVEY, MIKE
GASTON, JACK
GERARD, LOUIS
GIDDINGS, AB
GIDDINGS, HENRY
GLENN, ROBERT M.
GOODWIN, JOSEPH F.
GORDINER, C. W.
GRAHAM, EDWARD
HALL, WILLIAM
HALLICK, JOHN G.
HEATH, RICHARD
HENRY, W. J.
HOVEY, FRANK
HOWE, JOHN C.
HUGHES, CHARLES W.
HUNGERFORD, Z. N.
JENKINS, W. R.
KENNEDY, WILLIAM
KIES, JAMES HENRY
KIES, JOHN
KING, ANDREW G.
LAIRD, CHARLES
LAWRENCE, WILLIAM
LEWIS, CHARLES
LEWIS, E. J.
LEWIS, JOHN L.
LUCE, JAMES L.
LYNCH, JAMES
MACK, JOHN B.
MAJOR, JOHN N.
MARTIN, JOHN
MASON, JOE
MATHEWS, MILO
MATHEWS, WILLIAM H.
MAYHEW, WILLIAM
McCONNELL, CHARLES
McGUFFEY, JOHN
McGUIRE, MIKE
McINERNEY, T. J.

McMANUS, FRANK C.
MINTHORN, HIRAM P.
MONTGOMERY, ZACK
MORRISON, HENRY P.
MORSE, ANDY
PALMER, HERMAN C.
PARKER, E. G.
PARKS, ERSKIN
PRATT, NEWTON
PRATT, WARREN
PRYOR, ALFRED L.
QUADLIN, DAVID
REYNOLDS, JOHN E.
RICHARDS, GREEN
ROBBINS, DAN
ROBBINS, JARED
ROBERTS, GEORGE
ROLFE, CHARLES H.
SCAMMON, GUS
SMITH, A.
SMITH, C. V.
SMITH, FRANK M.
SMITHSON, JAMES S.
SPAULDING, ASHER D.
SPAULDING, MELVIN J.
STONE, RICHARD M.
STRAUSER, JOSEPH M.
SULLAWAY, JOHN W.
SWATKA, HARRY
TALBERT, WILLIAM S.
TICE, FRED
THOMPSON, FRANK R.
THOMPSON, JAMES
TURNER, HOWARD
TYNDALL, THOMAS F.
VAUGHN, GEORGE W.
WARD, HENRY C.
WESTON, HARRY F.
WILLIAMS, CHARLES
WILLIAMS, HORACE A.
WILSON, JAMES
WOLFLEY, JOHN
WOODS, JERRY D.
WRIGHT, JOSEPH

Almost 80 years after the first stagecoach rolled into Shasta, the Stage Driver's Monument was erected by Mae Helene Bacon Boggs, niece of Williamson Lyncoya Smith. It was dedicated in June 1931, in loving memory of these pioneers who "held the ribbons but turned the bend in this road." On this plaque, 145 names appear.